Laugh Without Fear

Laugh Without Fear

How to trust God with your future when your marriage falls apart

Shannon Jimenez

ADRIVANA PUBLISHING

Copyright © 2022 by Shannon Jimenez

All rights reserved. No part of this book may be reproduced in any manner whatsoever without written permission except in the case of brief quotations embodied in critical articles and reviews.

First Printing, 2022

For my two amazing kids.

You are the reason that I fight with faith, love with my whole heart, and dream as big as I can.

Index

PAGE 1 BROKEN

PAGE 6 MEANT TO BE?

PAGE 15 LOSE CONTROL

PAGE 25 WHAT JUST HAPPENED?

PAGE 35 LET GO, LET GOD!

PAGE 46 THE F WORD

PAGE 60 WHAT YOU HEAR, SEE, AND SAY.

PAGE 70 WHO ARE YOU WITHOUT HIM?

PAGE 82 THE GOLDEN NUGGET

PAGE 98 PRAYER AND FASTING

PAGE 111 IN THE MEANTIME

PAGE 124 NO FEAR, NO SHAME

PAGE 136 PRETTY EPIC

PAGE 151 BOOK RECOMMENDATIONS

PAGE 152 ABOUT THE AUTHOR

PAGE 153 ACKNOWLEDGEMENTS

Broken

one

As I stood there, tears running down my face, life moved in slow motion for just a moment. My two friends were in the car, waiting for me to finish talking. His sister was to my left, my nephew to my right, and his brother and other family members were on the porch. My husband stood right in front of me, arms crossed trying to stand still, alcohol on his breath, and the lights from the house shining right in my eyes, I could barely see him. I had said everything I came to say, his whole family was on his side, enabling him, acting like I was the one who was crazy. But at that moment, just before I walked away, I realized I was no longer angry. Hurt and broken? Sure. More than anything, I could feel his pain, he was guilty, ashamed, and afraid of all he had done. Maybe he just didn't know how to sit with his own thoughts anymore, maybe he couldn't handle the truth, but I just felt bad for him.

Looking at him this way, in this state, broke my heart. I didn't know who he was anymore, I didn't recognize the man I loved. The man I had built 10 years of life with, was a broken mess and so was I. I could feel the pain in his voice when he finally spoke up and said "can we please talk about this tomorrow?". Even though I knew we wouldn't be talking at all, I agreed and walked away. All I wanted to do in that second was hug him, kiss him, and tell him it would be ok. He would be ok. My heart felt like it was completely gone. Not just broken, but all together gone. It felt like the worst ending I could have ever imagined and I didn't know what to do anymore.

I mean really, what is there to do when this happens? How did I get here? How did our beautiful babies lose their daddy? How am I supposed to tell them that I don't know if they will ever see them again?

So here I am, using my pain, my trials, and all of this mess, to help YOU! I used to think that God let bad things happen to good people, but the older I got, the more time I spent in His word. I've realized that this may have happened to me, but only because God knew I was strong enough to get through it, and He knew I would use it to bring Glory to Him. One thing I know for sure is that the enemy tried to break me, he tried to shut me up, and stop my faith. He wanted to mess me up, but God decided to use all that bad for good. He brought me to this place right here, right now, so that I could help so many of you, going through something very similar. (Gen 50:20 NLT)

Before I can keep explaining what is happening, before I can tell you how my life exploded right before my eyes, I have to take you back. Back to the beginning. When it all started, a love that all started in a place I should have never been in, but I still believe it was all meant to be and I would do it all over again, but maybe just a little bit classier.

So get cozy, grab some coffee, and come on this journey, because it's a long and crazy ride, but by the end of this book, I'm confident that where you are now in your marriage and your relationship with God, is not where you will be. Just be patient, and do not, let the enemy make you lose your faith because I can honestly say that is what he wants. He knows he can't destroy you, so he's going to try his best to distract you and completely kill your faith, so that like me, you don't share your pain with anyone else. So that you don't glorify God. But I truly believe that God led you to this book, He chose YOU for a reason. God sends his strongest soldiers to the hardest battles. So if you think you can't handle what you're going through, I promise that you can. God knew that you were going to go through this before you even took a breath, but it's up to you how you will handle it. It's up to you to not give up on your faith, to stand strong, and stand firm on God's promises. When you think that he's walked away, I can promise you he didn't. The teacher is always quiet when it's time to take the test, just remember that.

You are so much stronger than you think, and with God behind you, there is no stopping you, as long as you trust Him. I know that it's easier said than done, I know you feel like giving up and walking away. When the whole world is telling you to move on, give up, get a divorce, date someone else, or whatever else they may be whispering in your ear, stand tall. During all that I've been going through, not knowing what God really has for my future, not knowing what will happen in a few weeks, months, or even years from now, I've had to let go of my own thinking and my own understanding and learn to let God do what he needs to do.

You have to give up control. Stop stalking your husband, stop begging him to come home, stop worrying about how you're going to pay the bills when he doesn't even call you back. I've been there, I'm there now. But God provides for His people. Don't be mad at God for what you're going through right now, He didn't make this happen to you, but He will indeed make this work for you. But you'll have to get to a point where you shut out the world's opinions and only worry about what He thinks. The moment that any of those negative or depressing thoughts come into your mind, push them out immediately. Those thoughts are from the enemy himself, they are his way of trying to knock you off course and trip you up. If you're sitting here right now thinking, What do I think of? What do I say instead? How do I get rid of those thoughts? I highly suggest that you start diving into God's word. Pick up your bible, or open the app on your phone, because sister, that is your weapon against the enemy. The more you read, the more power you have, the more you have to throw against the devil when he comes knocking in your thoughts.

If you are in His word daily, keep going, it'll only help you and open your eyes to what God wants you to see. If you feel like you don't understand anything that you're reading, just ask God to open your heart, and help you understand. Eventually, you will. I promise. But you can't defeat the enemy, and you can't conquer your circumstances if you don't have God's word backing you up. How do those words back you up? You read them and keep them inside of you. God's with you always, just like He's been with me this entire time.

So come back with me, to the moment I first saw my husband, to when I was in the wrong place, in a messed up state of mind, lonely, unhappy, depressed, drinking any chance I could, and as far away from God as I probably could have been. The moment everything changed and brought me to who I am and what I'm going through right at this point in time. The one decision that changed the course of my life for good.

two

It had been ten months since my ex left me heartbroken and I didn't take it very well. In my defense, I was only 20 years old and I had no clue what my life was going to look like anymore. Up until the point he left me, I just assumed that I'd be a military wife working at a hair salon on whatever base we would be stationed at.

My relationship with God wasn't really a relationship. It was more of an acquaintance. I'd go to church twice a week, and I loved Him with my whole heart, I just didn't know how to live for Him. It only got worse after I got dumped. I didn't understand what I had done wrong. I didn't know why my ex decided I wasn't good enough. I began to question everything I had ever known.

I started to spiral because I was so emotional. No one had really taught me how to be ok when my heart broke. No one told me how to react to my emotions, and to be honest, they were seriously out of control. I couldn't stop crying, I couldn't stop wondering if there was something else I could have done, I just wanted to feel okay for a few minutes. I didn't want to hurt anymore. So instead of turning to God and to prayer, I turned to alcohol, clubs, and a sad attempt at dating. It was a really bad 10 months. It was lonely and confusing, and I'd cry every night wondering who I was, what this all meant, and why I was even here. If you can't tell by now, I love hard....really hard. I have a problem letting people go, I know now that I had a lot to work on with my abandonment issues but at the time I was basically still a child and I didn't know any better.

Honestly, I think I spent so much time attempting to date a whole bunch of random men because I was so sick of being alone. I just wanted to be loved. Was it really too much to ask for? But God knew. He knew the choices I'd make, He knew I wasn't ready for real love yet, He knew that I needed to have a season of waiting. I just spent my time, waiting the wrong way. I tried to take my life into my own hands but that is something that I've had to learn not to do. It's all in God's time, not our own. No matter how much we want it right now, He will let us know when the time is right.

Now, my ex had left me in May of 2010, and the time between then and March 2011 was honestly a blur. I'm not proud to admit that but like I said before, it was my season of waiting, and God is using that bad part of my life for good. In March 2011 my best friend wanted to celebrate her birthday at this Latin club out in St. Louis. At this point, I had gone out so much that I was sort of over it all. I had been to a few clubs and it just wasn't my thing. I hated the music and I felt uncomfortable watching people in their 30s and 40s rub up on each other on the dance floor. Just eww! But she assured me this one would be different, that it would be like being around my family in Mexico. She was right, sort of.

It still wasn't the place that I should have been hanging out, but I drank lots of water and dressed in more modest clothes, and just had fun dancing to music that I grew up around. My stepdad is from Mexico and I had gone there since I was little, so the music reminded me of the fun I had there as a kid. Since I didn't get to see my family in Mexico very often, I loved the idea of going and being around that culture. By this time I was just done with chasing after men. I was over trying to be with someone and decided to just have fun being who I am. I was still trying to figure out who exactly I was, but I was in a better place than a few months before that.

So back to her party that night, I remember it like it was yesterday. We walked up into this different section at the club and she had seen this guy that she recognized. He was dating our old Spanish teacher from High School, and she introduced me to him. He was really nice and shook my hand, then he introduced me to his friend sitting next to him. This guy was clearly drunk and didn't care about meeting me any more than I cared about meeting him. But I was nice and shook his hand anyway. Growing up with a Mexican family, I was always raised to be polite and say hello, even if I didn't want to, it was wrong to be rude. So I shook his hand, barely looking at him for more than a few seconds, long enough to notice that he couldn't actually look at my eyes. He seemed like a dirtbag, but it didn't matter, remember, I was "over" guys at this point. I didn't want to date, I didn't want anyone thinking that I may be even slightly interested, so I kept my eyes down and I honestly couldn't even remember his name.

A little while later I was at the bar with my friend and she was talking to this guy, I again was so oblivious to the man standing there I didn't notice it was the same guy I had met earlier. I was busy paying attention to the people in the middle of the dance floor dancing so professionally to bachata music, I was almost in a trance. It was something right out of Dancing with the Stars. I had only ever dreamed of dancing like that. She had tried to get him to buy us both water bottles, but he refused to get me one because he had no clue who I was and obviously had no interest. I got my own water and then I decided that even if I was terrible at it, I wanted to try to dance like those people and have fun.

After a while on the dance floor, this guy kept coming around me and trying to dance with me. I had no clue what he was trying to do and in all honesty, I was just there with my girls trying to just forget about everything from the past year and have fun. So I moved away from him and continued the night with my friends.

Once it was time to leave, we headed to my car, tired and happy. I managed to go to a club, have fun, and not drink. Which was a massive accomplishment for me. As I closed the door to my car this random guy came up to my window and started talking to my best friend, asking for her number, saying that they needed to hang out and all that jazz, but the smell of the alcohol that was pouring out of him was literally making me feel sick. There was something about this guy though. It was, dare I say the most cliche thing ever, love at first sight?

Okay okay, it actually wasn't love at first sight. This was the same guy that I had met at the beginning of the night. The guy that didn't care to shake my hand, the guy that didn't want to buy me a water bottle. The same dude that tried to dance right next to me. I was in awe of him. Maybe it was too dark inside, maybe I was just tired from dancing all night, but I couldn't stop looking at him. I looked at my best friend and said "Who was that guy? He's super hot!" She looked at me as if she were slapping me inside her mind, and said "Really? You met him like three times and then didn't want to be on the dancefloor next to him. Do you really not remember him?" I honestly was sort of shocked that this was the same guy. So if you want to get technical, it wasn't love at first sight, but then again the first time I saw him I really didn't pay any attention to him. So the first time I really looked at him, I was hooked. There was something about him.

Looking back on that night, I don't know if that was the devil dangling a golden apple in front of my face, or if it really was God showing me my future husband. I'm fully aware that I shouldn't have been in that club, but I do have two beautiful children that God knew were going to come into this world, and for that, I'm thankful no matter what. We all have a past, we all make mistakes, and we are all broken at some time or another. The cool thing about God is that He uses broken people. He uses the messed-up lives to create amazing messages. He uses sinners to help others because He knows that they'll go places that "holier than thou" people would never walk into.

Maybe you're asking why I just gave you a glimpse into that night. Why should you even care about this girl that you never met and her story about meeting a drunk guy at a club? Well, maybe you shouldn't care, maybe this doesn't mean anything to you at all. But I'm more than willing to bet that you picked up this book for the sole reason of not knowing what the heck is going on in your world right now. Your life has probably been uprooted and ripped apart in so many ways you can't even see straight. Girl, I get it. I'm currently living that right now, and my husband stepped out 6 months ago. And thank God, that He has had patience with me, God that is, not my husband. God has really heard every cry, complaint, angry rant, and so much more and He still hasn't left my side. All of this, the waiting, the unknown, the trials, the tears, it isn't for nothing. I promise you that if you let Him, God will take what you're going through and completely change it around. He WILL do it, but not if you get in His way.

I was listening to Real Talk Kim one night and she said something that was basically a slap in the face. She said, "Stop trying to get ahead of God because when you do, He has to undo what you just did". Sometimes we really think we know best and man that could not be more wrong. All the times I look back and think how things could be different, I have to realize that it could be my own fault that they aren't the way I want them. I may have just jumped the gun and got impatient and got ahead of what God was trying to do.

When I met my husband that night at the club, we were both broken people. He was coming out of a messed-up relationship, drinking too much, and doing other things that he shouldn't have. He didn't know God even in the slightest and was drinking so much to numb whatever it was that he was going through because he couldn't handle being alone with his own thoughts and convictions. I, on the other hand, knew God but wasn't living the right way. I didn't know how to turn to God for help so I turned to alcohol instead. I was literally looking for love in all the wrong places and I was a complete mess most of the time. I'd go to a Friday night church service and go straight to the clubs or a friend's house and drink, and I would do the same on Saturday night and end up hungover in church on Sunday morning. No matter what we were both doing God knew how this would turn out. He had so much love and compassion for the both of us that He was moving in our lives in ways we didn't even realize.

I had never had someone like him in my life. He offered to pay for everything, took me out to eat, and opened the doors for me. It was mind-blowing because he was the complete opposite of my ex. I was the one who had to pay for everything with my ex, it was like he had no idea how to be a gentleman. God knew that I needed someone very different. I needed someone to take care of me. Here is the thing I've come to realize though, I truly believe with all my heart that my husband and I were meant to be together, but I feel like we rushed it and our timing may not have been what God had in mind. Like I said before, I didn't even like going out to clubs, but I kept going back week after week because that was one of the only places that I would see him. Sure it wasn't ideal, but he loved dancing so much and I loved seeing him smile. It truly lit up my heart watching him be so happy.

When we had finally started dating or being an official couple, whatever you want to call it. The way he asked me out made me so giddy inside. I knew I liked him, yes, but I wasn't sure I was ready to date him just yet. He was getting ready to leave a bonfire at my house and he walked up to me and this was our conversation:

Him: Will you be my girlfriend?
Me: What?!
Him: I want you to be my girlfriend.
Me: You don't even know me. Shouldn't we sort of date first?
Him: Yea, but I want to be the only one who gets to know you. So will you?
Me: *in a moment of weakness* YES!!

I don't know, maybe I was just so happy that he said it like that. Maybe I was afraid to continue being single. Maybe I was just tired after the bonfire. Really at this point who knows. Inside I was screaming like a little girl with a massive crush, so happy. So excited about this new journey. Little did I know how intense it would get.

That was ten years ago. I've seen so many reels on Instagram of people saying "If you could have seen your entire relationship before your first date, would you have still gone on the date?", I can't tell you how many times that question has played out in my head. Part of me wants to say no. I've been so hurt, cried way too many tears, had terrible fights, argued more than I'd like to admit, and regretted so many things. At the same time, I have 2 amazing kids, gone on so many fun vacations, had nights filled with laughter and fun, and so many amazing memories between just the two of us. I wouldn't take any of it back. Sure I may do it a bit differently. I'm no saint. But we can't rewind time. There was one moment a year or two after we started dating that I looked at my husband and said "I never used to go out to clubs. What if I never went that night? We would never have met, and we wouldn't have our little family." To this day his response still blows me away. When he spoke these words I knew that God put something on the inside of him. He looked at me and said "It wouldn't matter. We were meant to be, so we would have found each other eventually." This was straight out of a rom-com for me. I've never had anyone seem so sure of being with me. I knew this time it was different.

I just wish I would have been more prepared to be the wife I should have been. We can only learn from our mistakes and decide to do better and be better. God doesn't pick the people trying to act perfect. He chooses the broken, He chose me, and He chose you.

Lose control

three

Someone has to say it, so it might as well be me. We as women are some of the biggest control freaks in the world. I'm sure you're reading this thinking that you're not one of those women, and maybe you're the rare one who isn't. But I know for a fact that we hate not being in control. Between the kids, our food, friends, work, schedules, and especially our spouses, we constantly feel the need to be in control of it all, or else chaos may ensue. Now, this definitely doesn't mean that we are in control of everything at every time, but we sure do want to be.

I never really understood why I felt that need, but I knew it was there, and honestly, it still lingers around. As women of faith, we really need to learn to let go of control and let God do his thing. Yes I know, way easier said than done. It's hard to give that control up, even if we never really had it in the first place. Sister, let me tell you it is hard to come to that realization but it is so true, and it's a necessity in your walk with God and in your marriage.

I know that in the world we're living in, it's so popular for women to "wear the pants" so to speak. To tell your man you're not his momma and you're not doing his laundry or picking up after him or making him food. Can I ask why? Why is that such a terrible thing? Yes ok, we deserve respect as well and we love when our men shower us in love and cook and clean when we don't ask them to, but God created us for so much more.

In my recent separation from my husband, which we'll get to here in a bit, I've really learned a few things that sort of felt like a slap in the face. I felt offended, and I felt like I was losing control of my life and relationship. In reality, I'm not sure if I really had any control in the first place. Be prepared for the answers you're asking God for, because you may not like them. God is going to lead you to the truth, about you, about your spouse, and about what is right and wrong on BOTH of your parts. So here is something I've noticed after reading over 50 different bible devotionals, podcasts, books, and sermons about being married and what God wanted marriage to look like. One thing that kept popping up in almost everything that I looked into was this: Men want respect, women want love. It's kind of funny because we all know this, but we resist it so much. I know I did.

Growing up I always heard my dad yell about respect, and my mom would say that she wants respect too. So when my husband would say the same thing to me, I'd come back with the same answer that my mother would say "Well where is my respect?" or "You don't respect me" or even the classic "You gotta give respect to get it". Well, ladies, I'm here to tell you that we are wrong. I know it's sort of shocking, but hear me out. We don't really want respect, we want to be shown love. We want to know that we are appreciated for all that we do at work or around the house, or with the kids. We want them to share their feelings, cuddle us, and open up to us in ways that we open up to our girlfriends. So please listen to me when I say this MEN AREN'T BUILT THAT WAY. Look I'm not sure if it's because Eve was made from that part of Adam that felt like this, and it just lived on in every woman ever, but I can say that we are women and they are men. There is a reason that God made us very different. It took me way too long and my husband walking out on me, for me to realize that I was basically trying to turn him into one of my girlfriends. Instead of actually saying that I just want love from him, it came out sassy and condescending and I shouted it out as "respect" when it really wasn't.

If you ask any man, your brother, father, neighbor, or Joe at the supermarket, they will all tell you the thing they crave most is respect. They don't want to be told they aren't good enough, or that they did something wrong (even if they did), they want to be appreciated just as much as we do but they don't really know how to communicate that. So instead of trying to learn how to respect our men, we instead try to force them into respecting us FIRST when we are way out of line. Look, this is a hard reality to swallow, I know. I didn't like it at first either but when God wants you to know where your place is, and you are diligently seeking him for answers, you may just get put in your place. That's what happened to me one morning as I was reading through Genesis in my Bible.

I'm not sure what version of The Bible you read, maybe you use your phone, a physical copy, or even a mix of both. I do a mix of both, and sometimes I love the app on my phone because I can read one verse, and switch through translations to better understand. On this particular morning, I was reading the New Living Translation, and I was shocked at how it worded this particular verse, bare with me because if you don't read this version you may not like it, I didn't. It reads:

"Then He said to the woman, I will sharpen the pain of your pregnancy, and in pain, you will give birth. And you will DESIRE TO CONTROL your husband, but he will rule over you" (Genesis 3:16 NLT)

I read this, and I was like hold up what?!?! This woman not only gave us monthly cramps and terrible pregnancy pain, but we WANT TO CONTROL our husbands too? You guys, I was just as stunned as ever reading this. No other version puts it this way, but man oh man does it put so many things into perspective. We want to control these men so badly, but we have to realize that God didn't want that. He created us so that we could be HELPERS to our husbands, not the other way around. Yet here we are trying to get them to do everything for us, exactly how we say. We tell them "I'm not your mother" yet we want them to listen to every demand as if they were our son. Kind of messed up, right?

I get it, I do. I want love, I want appreciation. I'd love my husband to walk through that door after a long and tiring day and say "Thank you so much for how amazing this house looks, and for keeping the kids alive, and working yourself silly" but we refuse, and I mean absolutely refuse, to look at them and say "Thank you for working such long hours so I don't have to take time away from the kids." or "Thank you for doing the hard things so that I don't have to." Don't take this as me saying that our job is less than theirs. Girl, sometimes I think, why am I not getting paid a living wage for being a stay-at-home mom?! What I am saying is that we want all of this recognition from them, but they don't know how to communicate in the first place. Guys just aren't built to be sappy and great with words. Think about how your husband first hit on you, I'm sure it wasn't perfectly executed, and if it was kudos to you, but nine times out of ten, it's usually a macho mess.

Another thing I've learned about respect is that God wants us to give it to them first. Now look, obviously I'm not talking about abusive relationships here, I'm talking about good old normal marriages that have issues. We're human, we're going to mess things up, that's just a fact. As much as I want to hold my respect back until I get the love that I want, I've really been learning that God doesn't want that, and we shouldn't be that way, especially being the Godly women that we strive to be. Did you know, this is a bit crazy but stay with me for a second, that if you start showering your husband with respect, he'll have no choice but to give it back to you? I'll wait for the blowing of your mind.

Here is one way to look at this, if you have two cups on a table and they are both empty, your husband can't fill your cup because nothing is in his. But if you get up and grab that pitcher of, let's just say lemonade, and you start pouring into his cup, what happens? You start filling it, halfway, then it gets to the brim, then it starts to overflow. He will have two choices at this point. To start pouring it into your cup, or to let it spill all over the place. So if you start filling your husband up with love, respect, prayers, kind words, nice gestures, and everything else that God would be proud of, he will have no other choice than to start pouring it into you.

I know the exact question some of you may be thinking about right now. I know, because I thought it too so let's say it together "Why do I have to be the one to do it? Why not him?" If you are reading this book, which I'm assuming you are because God led me to write it, then I'm also going to assume that you may possibly have a better relationship with God than your husband does. Maybe his faith is stronger than yours, but then again if he was the one that left and not you, I'm going to guess that he may not have as much of the word in him as you probably thought. Sister, I get it, I want my husband to make all the moves, say all the things first, apologize first, apologize at all for that matter. But what if he doesn't? If we can sit here and teach our kids and even our pets to be kind and show others love even if they don't give it back, why do we think that we are the exception? Honestly ask yourself what is the worst that could happen if you show all of this respect and love to your husband first. Is it going to kill you? No, don't be so dramatic. It really comes back to all of that control that we feel like we need to have.

Now, I fully believe in standing up for ourselves and being the strong women that God created us to be, but that doesn't mean we get to take away the man that God is trying to create inside of our husbands. I've seen and met some amazing Godly husbands with strong-willed wives and I know they've had battles to overcome, but in the end, once we decide to relinquish that control and give it up to God, mountains will start moving in your marriage that you didn't even know existed.

This hasn't been something that came easily to me by any means at all. Not even slightly. I truly believe that God had to separate my husband and I so that He could work on us both because we are both stubborn. I'm still not fully aware of what God is doing in my husband's life, but I can tell you that he has changed me so much just in the past six months, that I almost don't recognize myself, but I do recognize how God is moving inside of me. In just a few months I've learned to forgive, without needing anything in return. I've learned to control my temper and think before I word vomit all over the place. I've been tested in my patience and majorly tested in my faith, and I know that it's because God is making me new inside and out.

Here is a fun revelation I got a few months back. I have to be willing to know what I am doing wrong. Let me say it one more time. I, and you, have to be willing to know what we are doing wrong in God's eyes. Not what your husband did wrong or is still doing wrong, but what we are doing wrong. This was really hard for me. I wanted to think I was right, about everything. Especially when it came to my husband. He left, he walked away, he is ignoring me, he won't come back around. Then one day as I was praying I remembered when David wanted God to search him for anything messed up inside of him that he needed to fix. He was sincere, he really wanted to know if anything was holding him back from what God wanted his life to be, and the blessings that he was going to have in his life. David said "Search me, O God, and know my heart; test me and know my anxious thoughts." (Psalms 139:23 NLT)

See, the thing is, sometimes we know we are wrong but we have too much pride to actually want to admit it. Other times, we really don't know how messed up our thinking is until we ask God to brutally pull it out of us. I finally had to sit up and be serious and really ask Him to show me where I was wrong, what I was wrong about, what kind of wife I truly was, and how I can start changing and be a true woman and wife of God. It's hard, really hard, to admit that there is a chance that I am the problem and not him. Now I'm not saying that your husband is perfect, or mine for that matter, what I am saying, is that maybe, just maybe, you had a bit more of a part to play in this separation that you are going through than you'd like to admit. Stop trying to control the way that your spouse reacts to you right now, and get right with God. Once I finally decided that it was time to stop trying to beg my husband to come home, and just work on my love walk and try to get closer to God and know him more, things started to shift. Not all at once, and not quickly, but once your heart really wants the truth, the whole truth including what you have on the inside of you that may be holding you back, then God will start moving those mountains.

Sometimes we are just so bitter about what we are going through we really have a hard time taking just a moment to stop and think about what it is that we could have done differently. Instead of saying "Well he did this" and "He said this to me" you need to be thinking "How can I change my reaction next time?" or "How can I speak in a way that would make God smile and be proud of me?". Stop trying to control your spouse, and start learning how to control your mouth, your thoughts, your relationship with the Lord, your patience, your self-control, your love walk, and your willingness to forgive. You all know the saying, when you point a finger at someone, three more are pointing back at you, or better yet "And why worry about a speck in your friend's eye, when you have a log in your own?" (Matthew 7:3 NLT)

When you start to give up the control of your husband and really start focusing on your relationship with God, not only do things start moving and changing, but God starts doing what He does best. God will worry about your husband. God will get through to your husband. God will start giving you revelations about things you didn't know that you didn't know. You may not like all that you learn, but our God is a God of truth and you better believe when the time is right, that truth will be shown. I know it's hard. I know it's frustrating and sometimes it takes longer than we want it to. But we have to start trusting that God knows better than we do and that this is on His time, not ours. If we try to get ahead of Him, it'll only prolong the wait. I promise you that if that happens you're going to kick yourself knowing that it could have been done after two months, but here you are two years later still trying to figure out what's going on in your marriage.

At this point, as I'm writing, it has been 6 months since my husband first walked out on me because of a fight that we had. He has been in and out since then for short periods, and every time I know that I've grown more than the time before, but I'm still not ready. God is still working in me and the control has been the hardest to give up. I want to know where my husband is at all times, why he won't come home, why he won't talk and have a real conversation with me. I want to force him to come back and see his kids, I want to control it all. But I can't. Honestly, this all could have probably been done with a while ago, but because of my pride and my inability to be told I'm the wrong one, God has had to sit with me a bit longer, and really show me what is going on and what it'll take to have my husband home again. Trust that there is a light at the end of all of this. Whether my husband ever comes back home or not, no matter if yours comes back or not, we have been brought to this moment because God needs us to work on who we are. The enemy wants us to believe that we should ultimately be the ones in control of our marriage, but wouldn't you rather God have the control? I can tell you from personal experience that God can and will give you more than you could ever give yourself or your husband. So do me this favor and read these words aloud, and really believe them as you speak.

I, (say your beautiful name), no longer want to be in control of my marriage, my husband, or my life. God, I officially give it all up to you. Lead me into where you want me to go. Search me for whatever it is that I am doing wrong, and show me how to be more like you. I don't want to be bitter, mean, angry, rude, or hateful towards my husband anymore. I want You to take control of my marriage and my life. I'm done with worry. I'm done with fear. I'm done with letting the enemy run around where he doesn't belong. I'm sorry God, for the things I've done, said, and thought, and things I don't even know that I did wrong. I trust you to guide me in this season because I know you are walking with me.

In Jesus name, Amen!

four

It all started with an argument over a stupid speeding ticket. That's how it always happens, right? The smallest thing will cause the biggest fight. The dishes didn't get put away and he left his dirty socks on the floor right next to the laundry hamper. She bought one too many packages from Amazon. At least this was what I thought that it started over, but in reality, this was the match that lit the pile of explosives that we were both apparently sitting on. The small things are what bring out the giant things that we chose to overlook as a married couple. We were both so convinced that we were each the most amazing spouse. He thought that omitting the truth about the ticket was ok, even if it wasn't intentional. I thought that I was in the right to call him out. That led to his attitude and me exploding in anger and using cruel words. Which in turn, had him walking right out of my life and not coming back home.

I can give every excuse to make it look like what I did wasn't so bad. I can blame him fully, and say that it was the heat of the moment. There was so much more than just the heat in this exact moment. We've all said it and we've probably all done it. Oh, don't act like you don't know what I'm talking about. That moment when we are so heated, upset, mad, sad, whatever emotion we decide to label it, and we explode and say things we don't mean. Women do this so much, usually, guys don't, and I don't know why we do this but I honestly think it's a defense mechanism. A little self-defense signal goes off in our brains, and we think that the only logical thing to do when someone makes us feel bad, is to hurt them as much as we can with words. They might be true, they might not be, but in that second we don't care. We only want to hurt them as much or worse than they just hurt us. Let me just be the first to say...STOP IT!!! We have to seriously stop doing this. It ruins relationships, marriages, and our walk with God. It messes us up more than the person on the receiving end, and you end up looking like the crazy person who has no self-control.

I know that sometimes all you want to do is fight back. When he yelled at me on the phone for my comment that I thought was harmless, I jumped at the chance to freak out on him, scream, cuss him out, and say things that I, hand to God, didn't mean one word of. I was just hurt. It took me way too long to see how that was wrong. My whole life, that reaction was normal. Women did it all the time. So why shouldn't I? Then I think back to that saying "Hurt people, hurt other people." When we are filled up with hurt and pain and only think with our emotions, we start doing things that hurt the ones we love the most. Was he in the wrong? Yes. Was I in the wrong? Absolutely. But this time, this fight, it was different.

I had handled other fights the same way so many other times. Different words, different emotions, different fights. I just expected him to come home, and we would get over it, not talk about it at all, and move on. Like every other time. I saw this quote by Dr. Steve Maraboli, and he said "If they do it often, it isn't a mistake; it's just their behavior." This was my behavior. I was kind to literally everyone else in the entire world. People have said horrible things to me, about me, family and friends, and even strangers, but I never said the types of things that I said to my own husband to anyone else. The one person I'm supposed to love more than anyone else in this world after God and next to my kids is my husband. Yet I repeatedly treated him like dirt with my words. Look, I'm not here to say I married the perfect man. He is far from that, but that isn't an excuse for me to talk to him the way that I had been for so many years. Remember in the last chapter how we talked about men wanting respect and women wanting love? Respect is not saying mean things just to hurt someone. Even if you feel like you've been betrayed.

What confused me more than anything else about this fight, was that we had only been back in our hometown for only a few days. We had just moved across the country, twice now in the same year, from St. Louis to Orlando and then back again. We were happy to come home. We were talking about our next step, possible house hunting, looking for a car, and our life back in the place I grew up. I could feel something was different the night we got back into town. I honestly thought it was just from being tired from the long journey with a U-haul and a minivan full of kids and a dog. We were all so tired. We were ready to be unpacked and of course, we were frustrated because the year in our new home in Florida, wasn't what we had expected it to be. Although I'm sure that 2020 wasn't what anyone expected it to be.

Just the week before, my husband was being extra loving. He had been in St. Louis, working, while I was back at the apartment in Orlando, packing up and getting ready for the long move. We either spoke on the phone or texted daily. I was stressed out with packing up and having both of the kids and the dog to take care of. He was back in St. Louis, working daily, looking for an apartment for us to come home to, and driving an hour to and from work daily. We were both at the end of our ropes, and we had a hard time functioning without the other. The day that he finally flew back out to get us and bring us all home was a day that I literally had a countdown for. I was so excited to see him and touch him in person. I couldn't wait for the kids to see their daddy. We were all super happy, to say the least. He started talking to me about not only how much he had missed me, but how this time away from me gave him perspective and made him realize how much he loved me. So much so, that he decided he wanted us to have a real wedding the following year (we got married in a courthouse with just the two of us and some random strangers we never met, so this was a super sweet thing for him to say). He was just so happy. Not that he wasn't in love with me before, but it was really showing and I was happy to be on the receiving end of his happiness.

So, as you can see, I was taken back by this fight that happened only a few days after we had gotten home. I was shocked that he didn't want to come back and work on our mess of a marriage. It all didn't make any sense to me. He dared to say that he loved me so much and that time had put our love into perspective, then was just ok with walking out on not only me but our kids. Who was this man? Did I really do something so wrong that he couldn't forgive me no matter how much I apologized? Did all of those things that he said just leave his thoughts? Did he lose his love for me in a week? My head started spinning out of control and I didn't know how to process this at all.

During that texting fight that we had, I told him not to come home. Yes, it was out of anger. I expected him to overlook the text and maybe stay with his brother for the night, but I never expected him to not want to come back home. I don't know if you are sitting there reading this and thinking "Wow, this girl is absolutely nuts, I'd leave her too." or if you are maybe saying to yourself "Ok is she inside my head right now? I know exactly what this feels like." Whatever your current thoughts of me and my actions are at this moment, just hold on to them, I promise things will get delightfully better and possibly a little crazier as we go on. My point isn't to say that it's all his fault or it's all my fault. But that sometimes, God will give you that little nudge, deep inside, in your spirit, and you'll know when something is off. You'll have that feeling of "Eh, I don't know, this seems kind of weird." That is what happened to me. I just didn't know it was God at the time. "But people who aren't spiritual can't receive these truths from God's spirit. It all sounds foolish to them and they can't understand it, for only those who are spiritual can understand what the Spirit means." (1 Corinthians 2:14 NLT)

God was starting here at this moment. He was trying to tell me something else was going on. I was just too hard-headed to see the truth. I was still stuck on "I didn't mean the words that I said, why won't he just forgive me already?" Looking back, I really have to laugh. God was about to rip the world I knew and loved, right from underneath me. I wanted my husband to forgive me so badly and just get over what I had said to him in the text messages. Little did I know that I was really the one who was about to go on a long journey of forgiveness and growth. God knew this all along, and He had been working in me the whole year prior, and it was time to put my faith to work.

I'm proud to say that I'm no longer the same as I was when that all happened. I'm not completely different in the sense of who I am and my personality, but when it comes to being with God, listening to what He truly wants me to do and how He wants me to react, well, that person is completely different in every way. I wasn't always the one who had the best discernment of the spirit. If you have no idea what I'm referring to when I say that, basically I had a hard time being able to distinguish the voice of the world from the voice of God. Not always, but it was definitely nowhere near what it is now. The night we got home and unpacked the truck, God nudged me, as if He was trying to tell me "Hey something is off with him, pay attention." I see that now, I wish I would have then, but I was slow.

Maybe you've been there. Maybe not this exact situation, but that moment that you felt God nudging you. That time that you felt something was a bit off with your spouse. Instead of listening to that still small voice trying to speak up inside of you, you just shrugged it off and went on your way. It happens, sister. We've all done it. Nothing is wrong with that. But our job is to get closer to God now so that when he decides to give you a heads up again, you will hear it, and you'll listen. I remember looking back thinking how slow I was. God was really trying to speak the truth to me, but I wasn't ready yet. And please, don't let this worry you either. If you are in a place in your marriage where you have no idea what's going on or what will happen next it's time to start trusting that God is going to fill you in soon enough. I've learned so much more than I've ever expected God to show me, but He is so awesome. We are so lucky that our God is a God of truth and justice. When someone tries to fool one of his children, rest assured that He will expose whatever the enemy is trying to do. Our part is simple. We have to trust God to bring us through this. If He can raise men from the dead, He most definitely will show you what is going on in your marriage that you don't know about. We just have to meet Him halfway. You have to believe Him. You have to have the faith, and continue to build that faith, day in and day out. The Lord's light penetrates the human spirit, exposing every hidden motive. (Proverbs 20: 27 NLT)

I of all people know how hard this can and will be for you. I know it's going to be easier to just accept that your husband walked out and think it's time to throw in the towel. Just like I'm sure that a soldier would think it would be easier to stay behind in battle instead of going on the front lines and giving his all. As I sit here and type all of this out, I want you to know how led you already are. Maybe you don't feel it. Maybe you don't see it yet. His hand is most definitely on you. These words are being typed up, on my 8th wedding anniversary. It's been over two months since my husband has seen my kids, and a lot longer since I had a real conversation with him. I know this is not going to be easy. If it were easy, you wouldn't want to fight for it. If it was easy, you'd brush it off and take it for granted. With full confidence, I can sit here and KNOW that you were meant to find this book. You've been looking for someone to tell you to stop running and start fighting. Well, I guess I'm that person. I'll gladly be in your corner. When the whole world tells you to run away and give up on the man that walked out on you, I'm going to tell you to stay, fight, and trust that God has a plan in all of this. I can't tell you that you won't get divorced. I can't tell you that God one hundred percent wants you to stay with your spouse. I will however tell you that if you don't start fighting for your marriage, you will lose it. I'll also tell you that you need to start getting stronger in your faith right now because maybe God has separated you so that you can learn to walk in love and forgiveness and learn how to fight the enemy instead of fighting your husband.

I know for a fact that my marriage wasn't exactly pleasing to God. Looking back on it all, on the bad anyway, I've realized that I no longer want that. I want a marriage where God is the center, not me and not my husband. I truly believe that He is working on bringing that to fruition as we speak. I've had everyone from close friends, to family, to even my brother-in-law telling me to leave my husband. I think that in a way it might be easier. But I really needed to ask myself some questions. Would it be what God wants for me? If I walk away, how does that glorify God? In some situations, it might, but I know that with my social media pages and everyone that I've come into contact with since all of this happened, deciding to stay, forgive, and really trust in God, that my friends, is how I can bring Him glory with my mess. Leaving isn't the only option, it's just the easier one. The worldlier one. Not always the wrong one, but you better make sure you are doing what God wants you to do, not what you want, and not what you think is easier and less stressful.

Don't feel like you have to take in everyone else's opinion on your relationship. I totally understand it. My friends want what is best for me and my kids. They hate to see me cry, they hate seeing me suffer, and most of them have already said the words "If I was in your situation, I would have left. I don't know how you are staying." I'm sure you have people in your life who are so amazing that they hurt when they see you in pain. I'm so blessed to have wonderful friends like this. I love that they love my kids and me so much that they just want me to be happy. I love each and every one of these people in my life. I honestly don't know how I would have gotten through the harder times without them by my side. Everyone has a right to their opinion, but opinions are just that, opinions. At the end of the day, you have to be the one living with, or without, your spouse. You have to be the one who knows you are for sure doing what God wants you to do. As much as I love these people, in the same way, that I'm sure you love the people who you have by your side, my relationship with God is much bigger and way more important to me. His opinion of me and my marriage trumps everyone else's a million times over. The people who love you the most usually give opinions out of love. That may not always line up with God's plan for your life. Seek Him, and look for what God is telling you to do. You never know who is watching how you handle your situations. Some are waiting for you to fall on your face. While others are just praying that this turns out so much better than what you are hoping for. He is a God of victories and miracles, so let Him do what He does best.

We sit here and expect and pray for God to give us a miracle, but we can't have a miracle if there is no explosion. We can't be rebuilt and made new until we are completely broken. That may look different for every person, but I believe that God is pulling you in a direction to be a warrior of faith, prayer, forgiveness, and love. This world is growing colder day by day. People are so quick to give up on the ones that they love. They want results right now and if they don't get that, they leave.

Honey, you're on God's timeline, not your own. Sorry to disappoint you, but He knows what would happen if you got what you wanted right this moment. I know that I wouldn't be ready for it. I know that God isn't finished building me back up. He isn't finished working inside my husband. I can almost guarantee if God did what you wanted Him to do when you wanted Him to do it, you would probably be right back in the same situation that got you here in the first place. Too harsh? Maybe. But are you truly ready? Sometimes God keeps things from us because He has to make us stronger to handle the situations that will come next.

I still feel like I was thrown into a twilight zone with what happened. Instead of asking "Why me?" or "When will you move God?" I'm learning to trust that He is working for my good. You need to start doing the same. You can ask 20 questions and still not get the answer that you think you want or need. *"For I know the plans I have for you…They are plans for good and not for disaster, to give you a future and a hope." (Jeremiah 29:11 NLT)*

five

Ok, so I'm sure you've heard the saying "Let go, let God" at least once in your life. I've had so many people say this to me growing up, but I never really knew what it meant. What about you? Do you know what it really means? It's like one of those sayings that we just like to throw around because other people say it and it really sounds good at the moment. Some sayings just make us feel good, but some really mean something huge. Like this one. When you hear or even decide to say this saying, think about what it really means. Let's look at the saying by section.

Let Go - Let go of all of your worries, fear, anxiety, anger, frustrations, sadness, and doubt.

Let God - once you let all of these things go, put them in the hands of God and trust that he will take care of it. Don't pick any of it back up, LET GOD take it all.

I want to take this time to talk about letting go of what you're going through right now and letting Him take care of it for you. I know it's scary. It's terrifying really. But it's oh so worth giving up and giving in.

I'm sure you're thinking "ok what should I let go of? There is too much, where do I start?" or maybe you're just at the point where you're only seeing red. Girl I got you. So we're going to start with anger. Yes, that lovely word that rips up relationships, always casts blame on everyone else, and makes you do the stupidest things that you would never have done in a normal state. Anger.

No matter why your husband left or decided to distance himself from you, you have every right to be angry I'm sure. Whether it be an addiction, an affair, or too many bottled-up emotions that either of you isn't really sure how to handle, money, or family. Whatever the reason, I know you already have an excuse in your head about why it's perfectly justifiable to be angry. I know this because I've been in this phase. Not only was I angry, but instead of driving through cranky-town just for a little pit stop, I decided to buy land and build a house on top of the biggest hill. It wasn't my intention. I didn't want to stay angry for so long, but the more I tried to justify it, the more things started to come uncovered, and the angrier I got. Then just speaking to him made my blood boil because he just wouldn't listen to what I had to say. He kept yelling over me. He wouldn't listen to or agree with anything I said. It was almost as if he didn't even care that I was so hurt.

Does any of this sound familiar at all? Girl, I bet it does. I bet you're sitting there right now shouting the word "EXACTLY!!!!" and nodding your head in agreement. Well, stop!! You have a right to feel the pain that your husband caused you, or maybe that you even may have caused yourself, that resulted in him leaving. But if you are reading this book right now, then you are in the exact spot that I was in, when I had enough. I was so sick of being so mad, but I felt like I couldn't help it. It was like I'd just wake up angry. Or on the rare occasion that I'd wake up in a half-decent mood, I'd try to call or text him and we would only argue and nothing would get resolved, which left me fuming. I hated it. It rocked me to my core.

I didn't want my kids to feel the anger I had inside of me, let alone see it. I didn't want them to think I hated their daddy, or that I was angry at them for anything that happened. Lord knows they had no part to play in this whole mess but they definitely felt the aftershocks of this earthquake.

It just seemed like the angrier I was, the less he cared to talk to me, and the fewer things got resolved. Even if he was just as angry as I was, it solved nothing. Anger literally does nothing for us. It makes us overemotional, we overreact, we say things out of hate and frustration, and it will set a fire that destroys everything in its path. Anger is so destructive.

Yes, you can be angry. You are allowed to be angry when you have been hurt by the person you love most in this world. If you're anything at all like me, you don't get too angry with anyone else, but man does that husband know how to hit every button like a Bop-It toy from the 90s. My husband hurt me so badly. Between a possible affair, the flirting, the addiction, and all of the wrong decisions he made on top of promising, word for word, that he'd never walk out on me, I was so angry. I not only wanted to understand all of these things and why they happened, but I wanted to make him hurt just as bad. That's what we do as women. "You broke my heart, so you deserve to feel just as much pain so I'm going to hurt you every way possible just because I'm hurting." It's like this sick joke that we play with ourselves. We start spitting out terrible things, we yell, we fight, and it gets to a point where we don't even know what we're doing or why we're doing it. All we know is that our goal is to demolish our spouse at all costs.

It's a seriously vicious cycle and the only one who can stop it is you. I honestly wish I would have learned sooner, but I know now, and honey I'm about to tell you the biggest secret of all. Anger is a choice. Yep. It's all on you, and I know that you really don't want to hear that. "But Shannon, you just said I'm allowed to be angry." Yes, yes I did. You can be angry. You can be hurt. What you can't, or at least shouldn't do, is act on that anger. Speak with that anger. Hurt with that anger. By all means, feel what you need to feel, you have to acknowledge your pain or you'll never heal. Then, let it go.

Look, I know this sounds crazy. God can't take your anger away from you. You have to be the one willing to let it go and give it to him. When you're angry, you can't have peace. When you can't have peace, you have a really hard time letting God fight your battles for you. When God fights, He wins. So basically, you being angry, means you lose.

"Therefore, dear brothers and sisters, you have no obligation to do what your sinful nature urges you to do. For if you live by its dictates, you will die. But if through the power of the Spirit you put to death the deeds of your sinful nature, you will live." (Romans 8:12-13 NLT)

If you want God to fight your battles, you have to be WILLING to let go of your anger. I know it's so much easier said than done. Look, I was angry for so long, I just knew at some point I'd just tire myself out and finally give it all up. I honestly wish I would have let it go so much sooner because God could have moved in my life sooner, and transformed me and my relationship. I think a huge part of me was terrified of the what-if. What if I let this anger go and he walks all over me? What if I stop being angry and he never comes back home? What if I let go, and then God does nothing? Those questions will kill you. The enemy lives for those questions. He's sitting back, thriving off of you asking those questions. Why? Because he knows that you have something inside of you that is so powerful, so amazing, that if you realize what you have, the enemy is out of a job. We serve an amazing God. A God who can literally move mountains and raise people from the dead. Yet we are over here, thinking that fixing our marriage, our husband, our relationship, or our hearts, is too hard for Him. It's kind of funny when you think about it. We get into that fight or flight mode, and constantly ask God "why me?", when we should be asking Him "Ok God, what do you want from me next?".

I've realized through all of this chaos, God has a plan, but sometimes we are just too thick in the head to realize that it's His plan, not ours. He will carry it out, and our purpose can't be stopped, sis. God created you for something so amazing, He wants you to fulfill it, but you gotta let go of your thinking and start trusting that He'll bring you through it. When we are so built up with being angry, it distracts us from all of the good. The good we should be doing, the good that we had, the good that God is doing right at this moment. Stop being distracted by your anger, the devil wants you distracted. He wants you so mad that you can't forgive, you can't walk in love, you can't be happy, and then you start to question God. Nothing, and I mean nothing, good comes from anger. Let. It. Go.

Let me give you a personal example right out of Shannon's Handbook of Anger. I feel like I've always had a short fuse, my entire life I've been so quick to anger, and I never really understood why that was a problem. My family was the same way, and maybe that's why it was so normal to me. Whereas my husband was raised completely differently. His parents didn't fight in front of him and no one really raised their voices. Mine on the other hand literally had fights that basically looked like screaming competitions. You know, to see who could yell over the other the loudest. It came second nature to me. If I was upset, you heard about it. I got mad. Very mad, and it almost felt like it was all the time. But I always hated the feeling.

LAUGH WITHOUT FEAR

Do you know how you hear of or see movies of women throwing plates, glasses, ashtrays, or any other random object at the man in the scene with her? When it's in a movie it's "OMG I wish I'd do that in real life" or "She's standing up for herself" or "YESSSS GIRL! Show him!" yea well in real life that was me, and it was frowned upon. Not by my friends of course. They laughed. You know who wasn't laughing? Me, God, and my husband. In the heat of the moment, I wouldn't think clearly, you name it I've probably thrown it or broken it, just to make a point. Ugh, I can't even explain to you how stupid this is. The worst part? I know I'm not alone. I know women personally who have done this. I know that some of you may have done it. I thought that "expressing" my anger if that's what you want to call it, would calm me down. It would allow me to not be angry anymore. It would fix things somehow. My husband just had to see how much I was hurt. He had to understand where I was coming from right? Wrong! He just thought I was crazy, and lost all self-control, and honestly, he wasn't wrong. In all honesty, I don't think I was ever taught how to manage my anger. Or at least manage it by God's standards. God doesn't want us to take it into our own hands, ever. Think of it this way. If you take your arguments, problems, or whatever, into your own hands, you may win, you may not. You're more likely to lose when you act or react the way that I used to, with anger. When you let it go, and place those problems in God's hands, ooooh girl! You'll win every single time. That's what is so awesome about God. He wants you to give up your problems. He wants to fight for you. He wants to win for you. But if you're stuck on the when, where, why, and how, instead of the who (God) and the what (letting Him fight), you'll be stuck in this never-ending cycle of lost battles.

It was best said by Miss Clara in the movie War Room "You've got to plead with God so that He can do what only He can do.

And then you've got to get out of the way and let Him do it!" We always think we know best. "If I could just get across that...", "If he would just listen to..." stop because you can't, and he won't. You can't change your husband. You can't change anyone, but anyone can change. Confused? Yea, so was I at first. No matter what we do, we can't change these men we are married to. In the same way that no matter what your husband demands of you, doesn't make you change one ounce. The more he pushes, the more you pull away. The same is true for your husband. The more you try to force him to see something a certain way, or think a certain way, or feel a certain way, the more that he'll do the opposite. Why? Because we have no idea what is going on in that head of his. We don't know what guilt, shame, or years of terrible teachings are going on inside of him. Do you know who does? God. God knows exactly what your spouse has to hear, see, feel, or do that will make him turn around and change. God knows how to fix any situation. Our problem isn't that God isn't doing it, or that He won't do it. It's that we think that we know how to fix everything. Instead of letting God be God and do his thing, we jump ahead of Him, block His way, and then create a whole new mess that He has to clean up before He can get to what He was getting to.

The way I see it you have two choices right now. You can either keep doing whatever it is that you're doing, texting him, calling him, pulling up to his work and arguing with him, begging him to come home, begging him to talk to you. You'll end up exhausted, at home alone, more depressed than you were when he first walked out. Or, you can give up this charade, wipe your hands clean and let God fight this battle for you. In all honesty, if you would have given up a while ago, God could have ended this way sooner. If I would have stopped being so angry instead of feeling defeated and frustrated, this may have all been over in 2 months, but instead, here we are about 7 months down the road, and I've finally learned to let go. Crazy how growth works huh?

Think about how far you've come right now. How has God taken you to a new place? How long has it taken you to learn to lean on Him? Now if your husband is like mine at all, he's not as close to God as you are. You are the prayer warrior. You are the one walking out in faith right now when everything looks hopeless. You are the one trusting that God is doing something in your time of suffering. Now, how long did it take you to get to the place you're in right now? One month? Eight months? Three years? Your spouse may take longer. God might decide to work a miracle and bring him back home to you tomorrow if you just stop being so stubborn. If He doesn't, you need to be patient and trust that God will bring that man home when the time is right. The lord is gonna fight for you babe, you just need to chill out (Exodus 14:14 NLT). No one takes a turkey out of the oven when it's still raw. So why would you want your broken marriage back when it's not done being cooked?

I really had to sit with that the other day. I had to come to the realization that God will do what He knows is right. So this is what I prayed, feel free to use it in your own life, but this really made me feel some kind of way when I said it. My prayer was, "Ok, God you're working on the both of us. I trust that you are going to help heal him before you bring him back home. I know you told me that this marriage is going to be unlike anything I've ever had, so I know you have to get rid of what I did have. God, don't bring him home until YOU know he is ready until we are both ready!"

Is it hard? You bet! I miss my husband every day. My kids miss him and it breaks my heart that they don't understand that daddy is going through a spiritual attack right now. He did some stupid things. I did stupid things. His may have been worse, but sin is sin. If God can forgive me, then who am I to refuse to forgive my husband?

I know that letting go of this control that we think we have, is the last thing we want to do. We don't want to let go of the hurt and the pain, but we want to have peace. We don't want to stop being angry but we want to be happy and whole. It's a bit redundant. Yet we still do it. He wants nothing more than for us to trust that He's got this. God wants to bless you so much. He wants you to have an amazing marriage. It's ok that your marriage might be broken, but remember God makes all things new. Just maybe, if you take a real step back and look at what your marriage was before, you'll see that it wasn't as perfect as you thought. Maybe it wasn't so bad, maybe it was awful and you just made excuses. Don't get too comfortable because God is about to take things to a whole new level, and you might not be ready, but you'll love what's on the other side if you would just Let go, Let God.

"But forget all that, it is nothing compared to what I am going to do. For I am about to do something new. See, I've already begun! Do you not see it?..." (Isaiah 43:18-19 NLT)

Sometimes we don't need to see the outcome. God likes to shock and awe. So I promise you that putting it all in God's hands is going to be well worth the wait. Then those people, who scoffed at you and called you dumb or naive for not giving up on your marriage, will see what you went through and how you come out on top, and it'll all be for the glory of God. You never know how your story will have a ripple effect with people who don't know God, and even some who do know Him. Honey, there is purpose in your pain, but not in your anger. So make a commitment now, to yourself and to God, that you are going to let your anger go and put all of this mess in God's hands. Let your husband be God's problem, not yours. Time to let go of it all, and let God handle it.

"I know how great this makes you feel, even though you have to put up with every kind of aggravation in the meantime. Pure gold put in the fire comes out of it proved pure; genuine faith put through this suffering comes out proved genuine. When Jesus wraps this all up, it's your faith, not your gold, that God will have on display as evidence of his victory." (1 Peter 1: 6-7 MSG)

So basically, God knows that a ton of people are watching you. He's not shocked that your spouse left, but He is waiting to see how you're going to handle it all. People won't understand when you stop being mad. I've had people tell me "I don't know how you're doing this Shannon, if it was me, I'd be so mad, I'd definitely handle it differently." Not just one person has said this, but multiple people with these exact words. The world looks at things differently than God does. The world thrives on anger, selfishness, and hate. We have to be different. We have to think differently. Why? Because we have God in us. So we need to show the world why He is so amazing, why we believe that He can do miracles, and why they need Him in their lives as well. When you live out your life in anger, you're giving the enemy exactly what he wants. When you decide to let that anger go, you move into the territory that God wants you in. That's when God starts to move, so much so, that people start to notice. People start believing in Him. When you react in a way that pleases God but shocks people, that's when you will start moving into a place of peace.

six

Alright, before you start turning your nose up to the title, rest assured it's not the word you're thinking about. Although, I'll go out on a limb here and say that you may not be as fond of this word either. The reason I'm titling this chapter "The F Word" is because just like the curse word that most people have to abbreviate down to one letter because they don't think it's right to say, this F word isn't much different. The word I'm talking about is FORGIVENESS.

As Christians, our entire faith is based on this word. God forgave us so that we could enter Heaven. No matter what we did, what we thought, or what we haven't even done yet, God forgives us. Forgiveness is something we want so badly, yet we have the hardest time throwing it around to others. Why is that? What's even crazier, is that the world would rather say the actual F word than actually forgive someone.

You may be sitting here thinking "Shannon, I forgive people all the time. I'm not against it. I know as a Christian I should forgive, so I do." Yea, I was there in that same spot once. I thought I was so good at forgiving. I had forgiven my family for abandoning me, my dad for choosing drugs and alcohol over me, my ex-friend for treating me the way she did when she had no right, the lady behind me at McDonald's who was screaming out the window and honking at me because she was having a bad day. I forgave them. It took more time for some, but I did it. I forgave, I let it go, I was at peace. I'm not saying forgiveness is easy, in fact, it's one of the hardest things we can do. It's something very easy to say, and very easy not to actually do. The whole world wants you to hold a grudge, but God doesn't at all. So even if you've forgiven your neighbor for letting his dog go to the bathroom in your yard, or your boss for yelling at you for something that a co-worker did, this territory of forgiveness is very different.

Honestly, this chapter may be the longest one yet. I could probably write a full book on forgiveness, but that's not what I'm here for just yet. I will say that this chapter is about you and your grudge with your husband. He is the person who is closest to you. The one you love and trust most in this world. He betrayed you and now I'm asking you to forgive whatever he did. "You don't understand what he did to me, I can't just forgive him. I can't let him walk all over me. He isn't even hurting like I am." Ok, so I'm sure some of these things are going through your mind right now if not all of them. I get it, I really do. I was there. I didn't want to forgive my husband. He walked out on me. He did things that shouldn't be forgiven. I had every right to be upset, hurt, and angry. I'm sure you do too. Well, get over it Sister, it's not about how you feel right now. That may seem a bit harsh, but forgiveness isn't about how we feel, how we were wronged, or what may or may not happen in the future if we do decide to forgive.

Forgiveness is a choice that we make because God told us to do so. Plus, when you don't forgive someone, especially your spouse, it holds you captive and hurts you more than you'll ever hurt him. He may want you to forgive him for what he's done, he might not care at all, either way, it's your responsibility to forgive him. Jesus said *"If you forgive those who sin against you, your heavenly Father will forgive you. But if you refuse to forgive others, your Father will not forgive your sins." (Matthew 6:14-15 NLT)* So in reality, it's your choice, but if you can't forgive your husband or anyone else for that matter, God can't forgive you. I don't know about you but that is something that is literally life-changing. I want God to forgive me. I'm a mess, and I know that I'll continue to be a mess no matter how hard I try not to be one. I don't know what kind of mistakes I'll make in the future but I do know that the ones that I made in the past I want to be forgiven. I'm sure you have things you're thinking of right now that you're glad God was able to forgive, no matter how bad they were. Yet right at this moment, you're struggling with forgiving your husband.

It's hard, trust me I know. At this point in this book, it has been 7 months since my husband walked out on us all. It's been 4 months since he has seen his two amazing children, or even tried to contact them or ask about them. I don't even know if he's thought about them. It's been 2 months since I've seen him and talked to him. The day that I realized that I couldn't help him anymore and that I needed to grow, not only in my faith but in my prayer life and in my forgiveness. I still can't understand fully what he's going through or why he really left us, or why it seems so easy for him to stay away from his kids. I wake up every day looking my little ones in the eyes knowing that I could never leave them, and he made it seem so easy to just walk away.

I look back at our arguments and I see where we both went wrong, where we weren't being good spouses, good Christians, or just good people. I've finally come to terms with forgiving not only myself, but truly forgiving my husband for leaving me, and for all the wrong he did to me. All the pain he caused brought me to this moment, it helped me see who God made me. But each day I have a hard time understanding how he could let these kids cry, how he could break their little hearts and not even care. I thought that I only had to forgive him for hurting me, that just doesn't seem to be the case though. I have grown more aware of the fact that there may just be layers to forgiveness. I don't know how many times I'm going to have to go through the pain of forgiving him for different things, but I do know that I HAVE to forgive him. Some days may be harder than others, and you can probably relate to me on this. Maybe your husband is doing the same thing to your kids. It's not their fault at all yet he's letting them feel like it is. Or maybe you don't have children, but he's still hurting you in other ways, even if you're apart. In my personal experience, he can still be living with you but not be there at all. I'm sure there are so many ways he has and may still hurt you.

It's kind of funny, at the beginning of all of this, when my marriage blew up, I really started trying to understand why I had to be the one to forgive. Why did I have to make the change when he didn't care? He hurt me so why should I be the bigger person when I'm breaking inside? Yet here I am telling you the same thing. I had so many different opinions, as I'm sure you've experienced as well. "You can't just bend for him every time." "You need to be stronger" "Don't let him off that easily just because you're a Christian" but what's funny is that I get it. I get all those things. He hurt me so badly, I felt like I was dying, truly breaking apart inside. 10 years of a relationship was completely falling apart. It was his fault. At least that's what I told myself for a while. Looking back I realize that isn't even remotely true. I could have done more, we both could have. God wasn't the center of our relationship or our marriage. We both had a part to play, and we both chose to blame the other instead of taking responsibility. I know how you feel and I know where you are right now. Seven months ago I didn't think there was ever even a tiny chance that I could be happy, or at peace. I haven't cried in over 2 months, and I wake up ready to take on the day almost every morning. I can't tell you how my marriage will end up, I can't even tell you how the end of this book will be. I'm writing what I am going through as I go through it. Every single day is a battle, spiritual warfare, and in all honesty, it's so hard sometimes. Each day is a chance for me to get better, grow closer to God, and really learn to give grace. The kind of grace God gives us every moment.

Sometimes when I see my kids upset and asking about when daddy will be coming home, I want to scream. I want to yell that I hate him and that he'll never see them again because he doesn't deserve to have that luxury after leaving them when they did nothing wrong. I don't want to be the better person, I want to feel what I'm feeling and not have anyone tell me that it's wrong. Jesus said *"It's not what goes into your body that defiles you; you are defiled by what comes from your heart." (Mark 7:15 NLT)* So if deep down in your heart you refuse to forgive him and you keep the pain and hate in your heart, how are you any better than him? Feeling those things may seem like a necessity at the moment. In the long run, those feelings will be what destroys you, not him. God pays attention to what is in your heart. He knows you're hurting sis. He hurts just as much as you do because of it. Just like how I'm breaking watching my kids hurt, that's the kind of God we have. He hurts when we do, but He sees the outcome of it all. He knows our future. He knows what's best for us. He will always watch out for us. If we decide to live with hate and unforgiveness, God has a hard time getting into our hearts and healing us. He wants to heal you, He wants to show you all he has on the other side of this whole situation but you're the one who is preventing that. It's not meant to be easy, nothing that is worth it is. Just like Jesus forgave the people who tortured and murdered him, we have to forgive our spouse for all the wrong he's done. Not because we are the Christian ones, but because they aren't.

My husband believes in God, sure. I'm sure he considers himself a Christian, just like most people do. Our faith comes from our relationship with God, not just a religion or a label. So if your relationship with God is a close and personal one or even closer than your husband's relationship with God, you have to be the one to see that. You have to be the one who can say and mean things like "Father, forgive them, for they don't know what they are doing." (Luke 23:34 NLT) You may be the only way that your husband makes it into heaven. I totally get that you still might be in your anger stage of all of this, so there is a chance you just rolled your eyes or said, "He's not my problem anymore" but you know deep down you don't mean that. This man that you gave your all to. The man that you fell so deeply in love with that you couldn't even imagine going through the situation that you're in right now, back when you married him. I understand that. I went through that.

I sat up for nights on end just yelling at God, saying "I'm not praying for him anymore." or "He deserves whatever happens next" and even "Just hit him with a lightning bolt or something". All of those things were said out of hurt, anger, pain, and sadness. Thank the sweet Lord above for knowing when we don't really mean something. God knows our hearts, he knows when we're hurting, and all those bad things we wished upon our husbands, guess what? He forgave us for even thinking like that.

Before any of you even try to think "Well I don't know if he will come back to me, and I don't know if our marriage will ever be repaired or restored, so what is the point of forgiving him if he never comes back to me?!" OOOOH girl! I know that pain. I have one hundred percent thought those exact words. I believed that they were totally valid thoughts. I was way off.

This whole situation has taught me so much. Looking back, I now know that there is a reason that God puts us in a season of waiting. We think we have it all together, we think that we know it all. We don't, and once we realize that, this process gets a little easier every day. God allowed me to go through this season so that I could learn and grow, and do it the right way. Sometimes the only way we can learn is over time and through experiences. So I want to share with you a few things that I've learned about forgiveness while going through my own struggles.

1. Forgiveness has absolutely nothing to do with the other person and is completely for your own good.
2. Forgiveness is actually a decision that you can make in a matter of a few seconds, even if it takes you a while to forget the trauma that it caused.
3. If you haven't forgotten the actual situation, that doesn't mean you didn't forgive them.
4. Forgiveness is necessary for us to heal, move on, grow, and make it into Heaven.
5. When you forgive people who have wronged you, it honestly blows people's minds. So much so, that they can't understand why you did it. That my friend, gives you a chance to give all of the glory to God, and in turn, leads people to Him.
6. People are watching you. They watch how you handle the situation, how you forgive, or if you don't, and how you come out of this. Sometimes they want you to fail and fall flat on your face, but more times than not they're looking to you for hope. Hope that they can get through their situations as you did. They want to see the good side, what happens when you don't give up, and that becomes the purpose in your pain. (We'll talk more about this a little later)

Obviously, I've been on a journey to heal and find answers. Most of us ask the same question "Why me God?". There is never a short answer, but there is always an answer. Your reason for this may be different than mine. When it's all said and done, you may end up in a different place than I will or your neighbor will. How you handle all of this that you are going through right now will, in the end, be how God shines through you. Ultimately it's your choice. It's your choice to heal, forgive, and move on. I can't promise you that your husband will be back in your arms by the end of this book, or even at all for that matter. I can however say that God absolutely CAN take everything that the enemy did to completely break you apart and restore it to better than what it was before. Maybe that's what He has for you. Maybe God is working on you and your husband separately so that He can bring you back together and you can be a holy power couple that makes hell tremble in fear. Maybe God is taking your husband out of your life because He has other plans that you need to fulfill.

We all have a different purpose, but we will never get there without forgiveness. That may sound a bit harsh, and yes you will be blessed and protected by God, even if it does take a bit for you to get to forgiveness. In all honesty, if you're wanting peace then you need to get on that forgiving train ASAP. Sometimes when we're so hurt we really don't want to do what God is leading us to do. For whatever reason as humans, we can be so stubborn about good things. We know full and well that once we let go and just forgive, we will be blessed with so much peace and healing, but it's like we want to just sit in that hurt for a few moments longer. No reason, just because. It's like when you were in school and you wanted to stay home sick because you knew you didn't have to go to school, even though you hated feeling so bad, you chose to stay that way and not take medicine anyway. What God actually has for us is so much better than anything we could create for ourselves. We tend to doubt that sometimes because we can't really see what it is that He has for us just yet. When you open that door of forgiving someone, whether they meant to hurt you or not, you also open the door for an insane amount of peace, and then the plan God has for you will become very clear.

Some people think that to forgive, all of their feelings about what happened to them have to be completely gone. That's not necessarily the case. It's a process. Like I said earlier, God knows your heart. So If you are willing to forgive and learn along the way, then He will bring you through all thoughts and pain that still need healing. We're only human, we're going to remember being hurt. Sure you may not remember what you ate for breakfast yesterday, but you'll always remember when someone wronged you. That's kind of how we're wired. But when the enemy decides to bring up those hurtful memories, you can either dwell on them and be bitter and hateful, or you can be forgiving, and take it one day at a time. It's always a choice, and some days may be a lot harder than others.

When our 8th wedding anniversary came and went, I heard nothing from my husband. I was doing pretty good up until that day. I was learning to be happy, I wasn't trying to fight him anymore, I was letting God do whatever He needed to do. But it still hurts. That doesn't mean I don't forgive him. I forgive him daily. I choose to forgive him. Some weeks I can go a few days without even thinking about my husband, I'm not really sure if that's a good thing or not, but I still pray for him daily. What I don't do is think about what he did to me or the kids. I just say a prayer for him, then move on with my day. A lot of my days have been like that lately. I'm getting to a new stage of healing the hole that he left in my heart. They aren't all like that but I truly believe that God is doing something great with all of this, and forgiving my husband helped me get to that sense of peace and trust with God.

I knew that I needed forgiveness, I just didn't know how to get to it. I kept hearing all these things about divorce, but I really didn't feel like God was calling me to that, at least not yet. As much as I've been trying to figure all of this out, I couldn't seem to find anyone who was going through what I was. Then I found this book called "Forgiving what you can't forget" by Lysa Terkeurst. If you haven't read this book yet I highly recommend you go get it as soon as you can and grab a highlighter, you'll need it. Lysa wrote an entire book on how she forgave all of her pain, and she had a lot of pain. For the first time, I felt like I could actually relate to someone. She was saying things that hit me like a dart and they were actually making more and more sense. If she said something I didn't agree with or I thought wasn't meant for me, the next few paragraphs would blow me away with honesty. Scripture after scripture backed her up in this book and made me look at forgiving my husband as a gift for me, instead of a burden. When I was reading this book, on the last page of chapter 2, I read something that had me in tears. At that moment, I realized, this is it, this is what God is doing through me. This is how I'm going to glorify You and bring people to know You as I do. Here is what I read:

When this world- so saturated with flesh resenting flesh, hearts hating hearts, fists slamming fists, pride rising against pride- suddenly sees someone dropping their sword and daring to whisper, "I forgive"...IT STOPS ALL.

In the split second of that utterance, evil is arrested, heaven touches earth, and the richest evidence for the truth of the gospel reverberates not just that day but for generations to come. While salvation is what brings the flesh of a human into perfect alignment with the Spirit of God, forgiveness is the greatest evidence that the Truth of God lives in us.

And none who sees this can walk away unaffected.

Wow, just wow. Mind-blowing, am I right? Reading that changed all of my perspectives of forgiving my husband. I'm not doing this for him, I'm doing this so that people see that Jesus is real. So that people ask me "wait, why did you forgive him after all he did to you?" and I can tell them that it's because we have such an amazing God that did that for each and every one of us. Do you see what God just did there? He took your bad and turned it into His extraordinary. What's even funnier, is that the same week I read those words in that book, I had multiple people ask me "Are you just going to forgive him?" and "Would you forgive him if he came back?" So many friends and family members asked these questions word for word.

It literally started happening so much that I started answering with a smile. I know weird, right? But that's when you get to see God working through you. You start to catch this little glimpse of the plan, you let a little smirk out and think "Ahh, I see what you did there". I'm sure He smiled right back at you and winked. It's all coming together for His good.

Maybe you feel like you've run out of options. I know I felt like that as well. I think there are definitely stages of how we go through all of this, the separation, the betrayal, the sadness, all of it. You have to allow yourself to go through it because there is definitely a reason that you're going to feel these things. Real Talk Kim said on her podcast once that you are going to go through your trial so that you can help someone else when they are going through the exact same thing. I fully believe that now, I didn't then, but now I'm like ok ok God sorry I was so slow, but I'm here now. Good thing He is a patient God. He knows when you're going to realize what is going on, He knows when you'll step into your purpose and into His plan for your life. Don't rush Him or the process. Trust me, the time will come and it all starts with you making the decision to forgive.

If for whatever reason you feel like "Ok well I did all of this, I forgave my husband, but I'm still not at peace, what's wrong?" then either one of two things are happening. You didn't really forgive him like you said. Remember, you can sit there and say all day long that you forgive, but it doesn't mean anything unless you mean it and believe it on the inside. If you're saying it, yet in your heart, you're still disgusted and hate thinking it, then sister you did not forgive yet. There is however another possibility, but it still involves forgiving. Look deep inside and see if you have something against someone else. Friends, family, a really annoying co-worker, etc. and let it go. Sometimes in order to move on in our relationships, other things are holding on to us, or we are holding on to them, and that is exactly how the enemy will get to you. He'll use whatever he can to distract you, don't let him keep you trapped in that place of not forgiving others.

Like I said at the beginning of this chapter, forgiving is a simple task, it doesn't necessarily mean that you forget everything that person did to you. But over time, as you pray, and forgive daily, you will get better at letting it go. You'll learn to grow and let God work on your heart. It's going to take time, you're human, and as humans, we tend to hold on to things. We remember the trauma and we remember being hurt.

I'll end with this, you have to forgive your husband. No matter what happened before, no matter what the future holds, no matter what he did or what you did. I know it hurts, trust me I do. But if you are here reading this book, it's because you want more. You want to forgive, you just might not know how to. That's ok. You'll get there. Each day it will hurt less and less because God is awesome like that. The devil wants you to sit there and feel all the pain and fill up with anger and rage because that's exactly what he did. But where does that get you? What does it get you, other than more pain? Forgiveness can only help you. And the world will never understand that. It's only natural to be angry with someone who hurt you. So when confiding in friends or family, they may not understand your choice to forgive. Jesus forgave everyone, even the people who still hate Him and don't believe in him.

Forgiveness doesn't mean you have to let your husband keep hurting you. You won't trust right away. You may still have to work on things with a therapist or a pastor. You'll have a while to go before your marriage and love can be renewed. Forgiving is the first step, and it has to happen for you to heal, don't resist it. I can promise you that once you open the door to forgiving, it'll start flooding your heart and you'll start feeling good. I can't say it'll be easy, everyone has a different situation, but I know for a fact that it is definitely worth it.

"I am not overstating it when I say that the man who caused all the trouble, hurt all of you more than he hurt me. Most of you opposed him, and that was punishment enough. Now, however, it is time to forgive and comfort him. Otherwise, he may be overcome by discouragement. So I urge you now to reaffirm your love for him...When you forgive this man, I forgive him too. And when I forgive whatever needs to be forgiven, I do so with Christ's authority for your benefit, so that Satan will not outsmart us. For we are familiar with his evil schemes." (2 Corinthians 2:5-11 NLT)

What you hear, see, & say

seven

We've all seen those little monkeys. You know the three cute ones and each has their hands over their eyes, mouth, and ears. Hear no evil, see no evil, speak no evil. I know that those aren't technically Christian, I don't know what they are honestly, but that's not really the point. I'm bringing them up because that concept will be so crucial to you during this separation from your husband and I can tell you firsthand that this may be one of the hardest things to control next to forgiveness.

Since we're not in Heaven yet, we're stuck in this world. A world that has demons running free, and people pay no mind to it. Some things will seem more harmless than others, and you'll make excuses so that you feel ok hearing, watching, or saying the things that you do. Honey, it's a car crash waiting to happen and you're in the driver's seat. Let's go through each of these by section and I'll explain what I mean by what you hear, see, and say. Before I do, just remember, if you're reading them and rolling your eyes, that means you need to work on them. I've been there, I'm still going through it now. The enemy knows exactly how to trip you up, and since God gave you free will, He is waiting on YOU to put a stop to it. God loves you so much that He'll do what He can to guide you, give you dreams, and put people on your path to help knock some sense into you before you destroy yourself. In the end, it'll come down to what you decide to do.

SHANNON JIMENEZ

What you hear- music, people, podcasts, etc.

I obviously don't know how you are when you go through things. Maybe you function well under pressure, maybe not. I'm assuming not so much since you're reading this right now, but in any case, I want to share what it is that I usually do when I'm feeling any emotion under the sun. Ever since I was a kid with my portable Walkman CD player, I'd drown myself in music. When I was happy I'd play upbeat music and when I was sad, it would be sad music. When I was angry...well I think you get where I'm going here. We didn't start going to church until I was about 11 years old so Christian music wasn't really a thing in my family until later on. So if I went through a break up I'd listen to songs about stupid boys, hating men, being strong, etc. Likewise, if I was crushing on someone, I'd listen to love songs. Que the eye roll, I know, It's pretty cliche but what can I say. I've always felt every emotion super intensely. Some people are like that, some aren't. On the off chance that you're not that way then this part may not be too hard for you to control. You might be ok with things you're listening to, and that's amazing, more power to you. I'm definitely not like that though.

Earlier last year, I decided to get away from secular music, if you have no clue what that is, basically music that's not Christian music. Music that's worldly. It was my personal decision, no one forced me or told me to, but I noticed that my mood, my prayers, my daily life, was just better when I only listened to Godly music. Do you have to do this? No. Will it make a difference in your life and relationship? Yes. That goes both ways. Once my husband left I started listening to Taylor Swift songs, you know the ones, about how dumb her exes were and are. They made me feel empowered...for a little bit. Then that started to transition into other songs and me feeling other ways. I stopped listening to Christian music almost altogether and I started feeling like there was no point in my marriage anymore. Why even bother with a man who walked out on me? Why should I pray for him, I doubt he prays for me. Maybe I should start dating other guys, maybe I'll find someone else even better. All of these were thoughts that I had in my head. The enemy used music to push me away from what God wanted me to do. It started to draw out the process of my healing, and I started to build up resentment and anger towards my husband, and honestly towards all men. Men who never even did anything to me, just because they were men. Now ladies, just because the world says that all men suck, does not mean that it's true. God has a lot of men out there who are good, amazing, kind men. I know it seems like there aren't any, or that maybe all the ones you've come across aren't really great but that's not the case for every guy out there.

When you start relying on music to make you feel a certain way, many things can change. I mean that in good ways and in bad ways. Maybe you've never listened to a worldly song in your life, fine. Then you're one step closer to fixing your marriage. On the off chance that you're like me, blaring Demi Lovato's Sorry Not Sorry in the car, it's time to change some things, sis. Music is so powerful. It affects us on a deep level because we feel the emotion behind it. We connect with the words that the artist is singing, and we feel like someone out there knows exactly what we're going through. We don't feel so alone anymore. I get it, I really do. In all reality, we're not alone, we just think we are. God knows exactly what you're feeling. He knows that you cry yourself to sleep at night, and you have a hard time driving by the coffee shop on your way to work every day because that's where you and your husband used to go every Sunday after church. He knows what you feel, what you wish would happen, and what you are praying and begging for. He also knows your husband's side. He knows what your husband is going through at this moment, what he is feeling, and if he's praying at all. Once you start shutting out God's music and start trying to "feel something" with secular music, things can start to go downhill really quickly. I'm telling you this from personal experience. And it's hard, I get it, but it's a little easier day by day when you listen to what God wants you to hear. You'll get stronger, and most likely some answers that you've been praying for.

This may sound funny to you, but sometimes I listen to music because it's what I WANT to feel, or hear, it's not about the hard truth and what I NEED to hear. Just like when you have someone close to you trying to give you the truth, it isn't really what you want at that moment, but you definitely need to hear it sometimes. That's how God is with his music. Music is so powerful, and our God knows that without a doubt. He knows how it can change your thinking, your strength, your worries, fears, etc. So think of it this way, if God knows that music will affect you so deeply, then the devil knows that same thing as well. The enemy will try to push any other music on you, and it might be the opposite of what you're supposed to be hearing.

What I mean by this is, to say that God wants you to trust your husband and eventually work on restoring your relationship. The enemy is going to give you songs that remind you of his infidelity, lies, all his sins, and mistakes, and you're going to hear songs about "strength". I put that word in quotes because worldly strength is different from God's strength. The world will tell you that you need to be a strong single woman who doesn't need a man, and you shouldn't do his laundry, and you should party and be single forever. When God will say, No, you should be there with him because he makes you whole and you'll fulfill my plan for your life only if you're a Godly couple. You must walk out of this life together.

What we allow inside our minds and hearts can deeply affect how we act, who we become, and whether or not we decide to listen to God. I'm not saying you can never listen to a secular song ever again, that's between you and God. What I am saying is that right now, being vulnerable to the enemy's attacks, it's a better idea to stay closer to God than the world. Try it for a week, make a playlist on Spotify, or listen to the Christian radio station in your area. Just take it one day at a time and try to only allow yourself to listen to Godly music or podcasts. Don't waste time listening to women ranting about how they don't need a man, or how it's better to go party and do it all alone. I promise that you'll see a difference. Once you get to the end of your first week, try another, and another.

What you see- movies, tv, youtube

So this may sound repetitive, and it kind of is, but I feel like it needs to be said or else you'll find a way out of it. That's how my mind works anyway. I always try to find the loophole. This is basically the same thing as minding what you listen to. When you watch certain things it can adjust your perspective, be it good or bad. So try to watch shows, movies, or YouTubers that bring light into your home.

I know for a fact that not everyone reading this book is the picture-perfect model Christian. None of us are, so before you get offended by me thinking that you watch things you shouldn't, know that we all do. It's ok to be human. I never used to think that something you watch could really affect what spirits come into your house, or how your mood can change. So maybe you don't watch horror movies, cool. Maybe you watch PG-13 movies from the early 90s because you grew up on them and you've seen them more than a million times. Maybe they aren't really "bad", but there are a few cuss words here and there, and maybe the main character is constantly telling her boyfriend not to control her, or something like that. I don't know what you watch, but you do. Judge yourself wisely, really take a step back, and think about what you watch and why. Try to find streaming services that are Godly, there are definitely a few. Find YouTubers that don't say bad things and that talk about God in their videos. They are out there, even if it seems like there is only trash on the web. The Chosen is an awesome series to watch as well and it's free, so if you haven't watched that yet I highly suggest you do. You'll feel like you really know Jesus more and more and it'll have a really good influence on your current situation.

Try finding other pastors to listen to as well. I know some people refuse to listen to anyone other than who speaks at your church, but there are some great people who have such a gift from God, and when you find them, you'll see that they're a gift to you.

Lastly, watch what you say

Ok so this may seem a little weird being put in this category, but there is definitely a huge reason why I'm making sure I talk about it. This isn't necessarily about you saying bad words or having an attitude, yes be careful with those but this category is a bit different. I learned this one the hard way.

In the previous chapters, you all learned that my mouth was what started this whole mess in the first place. Honestly, sometimes I think we would all be better off as mutes. We get into such a deep hole with what we say, sometimes it's hard to get out of it. Luckily God knows our hearts, He knows when we mess up and say stupid things that we don't mean, and hurt the people we love. I've already touched on you speaking to your spouse differently, but this isn't that.

As women, we have a pack of other women behind us. Our sisters, cousins, mothers, best friends, basically an army of women ready to come to our defense. Most of the time, that means we rip apart these men, and we do it together. We talk about how terrible they are, how dare they leave us with everything they've done, they're trash and we should just tell them off. Do you catch my drift?? Then they start chiming in with "I knew he was a dog." and "He messed up, he's just trash" and you nod your head and agree with every word. Well sis, sorry to burst this huge bubble, but it needs to STOP!! Now. I know, it's just you venting, you want their support, you want to feel like someone is in your corner I get it. I did this, and my friends did this. It's normal. You've either done it or been around it your whole life. I know I have. So when I was doing a devotional and reading about being a Godly wife, I was completely shocked that this was something bad that I was doing. I never cared if someone called my husband a bad name if he was being terrible. I'd always come to his defense if it was random and they just didn't like him, but when he messed up, ooh did I let them rip him up. I figured it was justice, he deserved it and I encouraged it. They were just protecting and defending me, right? Wrong.

Here is what actually happens. When you start speaking bad things about your relationship, and over your husband, what you are really doing is confessing those things about him. True or not. In the beginning, you were so in love with him, begging God to bring him home, wanting answers, and not knowing what went wrong. Then the whole girl gang went to town for the sake of this man's name, and they now have all of these images that they think are accurate, when in reality, they don't even know the whole story. God decides you're ready to get back together, but now, your mind and heart are starting to shift, and your friends and family think your husband is the worst possible outcome for you. So instead of listening to God, who not only fixed your husband, brought him back home, and answered YOUR prayers, you're starting to listen to these women because of what you allowed them to say over him. I know it's hard, but talking bad about someone is wrong, even if that someone is your husband who walked out on you.

Think about the times that you have messed up. Did God sit there and say that you were terrible, unforgivable, unloveable trash, and a mess? No, absolutely not. He said that you are worthy. No matter what you did, and still might do. He didn't talk bad about you, so watch what you say. I get wanting to vent, but sometimes we will vent and our loved ones will start saying whatever they want. You will have to be the one to put a stop to it. Do it respectfully, but do it nonetheless. I had to do this with a few friends, and once I explained what this meant to me and why they understood and they were more kind and careful of what they spoke.

Here are some verses that go along with what you speak.

- "The spirit of the Lord speaks through me; His words are upon my tongue." (2 Samuel 23:2 NLT)
- "My lips will speak no evil, and my tongue will speak no lies" (Job 27:4 NLT)
- "Those who control their tongue will have a long life; opening your mouth can ruin everything" (Proverbs 13:3 NLT)
- "Watch your tongue and keep your mouth shut, and you will stay out of trouble" (Proverbs 21:23 NLT)

These are just a few, but the bible is full of verses that touch on speaking and how it can affect your prayers, life, and outcome of everything. You are in control of what you listen to, watch, and say. It may seem like you aren't at times, but God isn't going to let you walk into something that you can't control, but He may just test you to see what option you choose. There will always be the temptation to give up, and just do whatever you want. It'll feel better to tear apart your husband's name because of how he hurt you. It's freeing to listen to songs that make you feel empowered and make you feel like you don't need any man ruining your life. That you're better off alone, not loved, and independent. You'll want to bury yourself in movies and shows that make you forget that you ever had a husband, or that love even exists. It will absolutely be so much easier to take that road. It'll hurt so much less and you won't have to fight to keep your head up. Is that worth it for you though?

Maybe you think that God gave you too much to handle but it's quite the opposite. The only reason that all of those things will be so much easier is that the enemy doesn't want you fighting against him. Not only is the devil a lazy punk, but he knows that if he can keep you away from fighting, really fighting the way that God wants you to, then you will give up and you'll never get to the purpose that God has for you to fulfill. Stay in it a little longer. Fight a little harder, feed your soul all of the goodness that God has to offer. I'm pretty sure if you step back for just a moment you'll see that there is always an option to do it God's way or to do it the world's way. You'll always have a choice. Pick the right one, even if it's hard at first. You'll be glad you did.

Who are you without him?

eight

Okay, so I have a bit of a loaded question, but it is a serious one that you need to think about. Well, I guess it's more like two questions all wrapped into one if I'm being honest. I want you to sit down in front of a mirror, or close your eyes and really ask yourself "Who am I without HIM?". Because this is a really difficult time in your life you need to know two things. Who you are without your husband, and who you are without God.

Now maybe this seems a bit silly, or redundant. I just wish I would have asked myself this at the beginning. I didn't think I needed to know who I was. I thought I already knew. Honey, one way or the other you're going to have to come up with the answers to these questions. It's way better to answer them now before you go and self-destruct.

"Why would I be self-destructive Shannon? That doesn't make any sense, I know that I need God more than ever right now, and my husband is the one who destroyed the relationship..." Yea, ok, let's start by getting you off that very high horse you're riding around on. I truly believe, now more than I ever have before, that you are literally learning from my mistakes. I was meant to write this book for you because of what I went through, and am still going through. I'm honest to God writing this as I'm going. As I'm messing up, making mistakes, learning, and growing. I've never written this much on one topic in my life, I mean it was hard enough to write a 5 page paper in High School, and now here I am writing a book. It's weird how God will lead you once you listen. Then again, that is probably why I'm here in this situation anyway. I didn't want to listen. I didn't want to wait. I was so sick of being patient, and not knowing what was going to happen that I truly believed that I knew better than God. I thought that I could just make things happen. Man, He must be sitting up there in Heaven laughing and shaking His head, knowing what was awaiting me. Knowing that I'd stumble and then come crawling back to Him. The reason I said you need to get off of your high horse, is because I was on mine. I didn't think that I'd stumble, or completely get distracted but I did. Why? Because I didn't ask myself who I was without God, and who I was without my husband.

Let's start with asking ourselves about who we really are without our spouse. When you are with someone for so long, you start to become one with them. They start acting like you, you start saying the same phrases and liking the same foods, and you change a little, or sometimes a lot. That's not necessarily a bad thing, but once that person walks away, it tends to leave a big hole in your mind, body, and soul. Maybe you were married for ten years, maybe just one, either way, you feel empty. This is because when you get married, in God's eyes, you become one. *"This explains why a man leaves his father and mother and is joined to his wife, and the two are united into one." (Genesis 2:24 NLT)*

When you are one, and one walks out on the marriage, you literally break in half. Half is then never whole. See where I'm going with this? Society, friends, family, and who knows who else will say that you're being dramatic. Not to God. He knows how broken you are. He didn't intend for marriages to end. So you're not being crazy when you feel like you have no idea who you are anymore. Maybe you feel like you have no purpose, or you're lacking passion. You need to learn to be able to redirect that in a positive and godly way.

You will naturally try to feel whole again, and sometimes that means filling that void with alcohol, partying, maybe even something as simple as binging TV. You think you need to feel something, that you need to "figure out who you are" so that you can move on and have a life. Everyone will tell you to move on, grow, have some self-care, and find yourself.

When I was with my husband I felt whole. I felt like I really didn't need anything else in my life. I was content. Once he left it felt like my whole world fell apart and I lost who I was. I've always been me, but when I got married, some of my personality, career goals, and life all started to change. Not intentionally, but they did nonetheless. So when that rug was ripped from under my feet I felt like I was completely exposed and ashamed. I wanted, no, I needed to find out who I was without him. You'll feel that way too and it's ok. It's normal. Just be very aware that you can channel that positively or negatively. If you choose the negative route, it can break you, and wreck the plans that God has for your future. Just like I stated previously, you need to let go and let God, but you can't really do that if you're running around being destructive. Take it from me, don't be stubborn. It's not worth it, and when you get distracted from what God is trying to get you to see, He will disturb what actually has your attention, and it'll hurt.

While it's great that you want to go on this journey of self-discovery, remember something, you are a child of God. I know it's funny to think that because you obviously know you are. You love being a child of God, and you know that you won't walk away from Him. Or will you? We think that we got this. We think we can handle anything that gets thrown our way, but sometimes, it's not that we can't handle it, it's that we just don't want to handle it. We think we know what's best for us, but even Peter denied Jesus, and he claimed that he wouldn't. You're not above any of this, and I wish someone would have knocked some sense into me before I thought I could do it on my own.

That actually brings us to the next question. Who are you without God? Once you start searching for who you are without your husband, you may end up on the wrong side and not really knowing where you're going and if you're taking God with you.

I've been a follower of God since I was little, but that didn't separate me from the enemy's trap. You will get distracted, angry, frustrated, stressed, desperate, and hopeless, when you're going through major tests. That's exactly what the devil wants. That isn't what God wants for you though. I was reading a book recently by John Bevere and he said something that really stuck with me. He said, "In serving God, there is always a testing period. We are tested in obedience before we are appointed or anointed". This sentence really hit me. God is going to guide you to do amazing things, to your calling, but only after He knows that you are wanting to do His will. After He sees that you are willing to be obedient to him. I get that now.

For a while, I was just over it. I didn't want to wait anymore. It was annoying to have to talk about my husband like he was here, or like he was actually trying to make any effort in our marriage when the reality was that he was completely absent. I was tired of waiting for the promises that God had given me about my marriage. I started to doubt it all. I started questioning everything. Did I really hear correctly from God? Was that dream God or me? Was that specific sermon really meant for me to hear, or was it for someone else that day? Then, of course, I started with thinking "well if God wanted us together then my husband would just be here, he'd show me he's changing." Girl, I can't tell you how messed up those things got me. The enemy WILL distract you until he either knocks you off course, or you stand your ground and let him know that you are waiting on God. PERIOD.

When God has a huge plan for your life, honestly any plan at all for your life, the attacks will come. No one ever said that being a follower of Christ would be easy. God isn't a genie that is here to make your life simple because you asked Him to. It's cute that some people think that way. No, when you follow the plan that God has for your life, hell knows that things will get shaken up for the glory of God. It's been said before, so I'll say it again, thieves don't rob empty homes. If you didn't have a bigger purpose, the enemy would not care at all about you or your spouse. Sure I've heard people say this, but it was like I forgot it for a while and then just didn't care. I was so sick of the attacks, I didn't think I was strong enough. Maybe you have been thinking this as well lately. Why me God? Why can't this happen to someone else?

I get it, but babe, you were chosen. Chosen as someone that God knew would move mountains and make earthquakes. God knew you couldn't do it alone. That's why you need Him. He is the one that gives you the strength to keep going, to do the unimaginable, to fight that massive fight of faith when everyone else is telling you to give up and go home. When you don't have Him in your corner it'll be way easier to fall flat on your face. You might be yelling out to God "I CAN'T DO THIS ANYMORE, I JUST CAN'T!" And honey you're right, you can't. Not without Him. I'm going to give you a few verses that'll show you that He is right here with you. I know it's hard to go at this alone, so don't. Go at your situation head-on, with God right by your side. Sometimes we just need some reminders that He's here with us when we feel alone, when we feel like we just can't go one more day, and when we feel like all hope is disappearing.

- So do not fear, for I am with you; do not be dismayed for I am your God. I will strengthen you and help you; I will uphold you with my righteous right hand. (Isaiah 41:10 NLT)
- I can do all things through Christ who strengthens me. (Philippians 4:13 NLT)
- For God has not given us a spirit of fear and timidity, but of power, love and self-discipline. (2 Timothy 1:7 NLT)
- Seek God's will in all that you do and He will direct your path. (Proverbs 3:6 NLT)

God wants you to trust that He is doing things for the better. It might seem so hard right now but think back to when you were younger. I remember when I was 12 or 13 years old and a boy didn't like me, or worse, a boy dated me for a bit then broke my heart. At that time, that was the worst heartache for me. I didn't think I'd ever get through it. I thought it was too hard, not fair, and I didn't see how any of this made sense. I constantly asked God why. But now, in my 30s, I look back and I can laugh. It seems so trivial. I'm sure you have something that's similar to that, something that you can look back on and think "wow was that really that bad?!". Right now, what you are going through with your spouse seems like the hardest thing you've ever had to go through. Maybe it is, maybe it's not. It seems so terrible because it's your season right now. You are meant to go through certain things, no matter how hard.

In John Bevere's book Multiply your God-given potential, he says this about moving into where we are meant to be in God's plan. "He will not show you every step at the beginning or even two or three steps ahead. It would have been so much easier to look into a crystal ball...however, if that had been possible, we wouldn't have contended for each step so intensely in prayer and leadership. Also, we would not have acquired the faith and strength of character that occurred with each step of obedience. All you have to do is pray, listen, believe, and obey what He puts in your heart."

I loved reading this because if we just got to coast through life, taking it easy, then we wouldn't be able to become the person God needs us to be for our calling. There is no way that I would be able to write this book if I was still in Florida, enjoying life at DisneyWorld all day with my kids and being with my husband. He had to leave, we had to go through trials, I had to learn to lean on God with all of my understanding. Sometimes when faith is the only thing you have left in your life, that is when your strength starts to push through. I can honestly say that if my spouse and I hadn't gone through the things we're currently going through, I would NOT be as strong in my faith. I wouldn't be diving into God's word on a daily basis. I wouldn't be trusting God for the hard things because I wouldn't have hard things to trust Him for. Sure I wish things would have worked out a little differently, but I'm also thankful for the strong woman of faith that I've become and am still growing into. I wouldn't take this experience back even if God gave me the chance to. I love the woman that I'm becoming. I love that my kids are seeing a very strong mother, standing in her faith, relying completely on God to take care of everything. That is teaching them more than they even realize at this moment. I'm showing them that I NEED God to get through the hard times, that I can't do it alone. Without God, I'm nothing. As hard as that is to realize, it's beyond true.

Sometimes we think that we can do it all by ourselves. Well, sorry to disappoint but we can't. When I stepped away from God for a brief moment because I thought I knew best, I backtracked. I started to self-destruct. I started getting distracted, not caring, not following the calling for my life and doing things I always said I wouldn't. Why? Because I'm human, and when we're left alone we make huge messes. With God by our sides, that's when we flourish. That is when we make waves.

Jesus didn't just sit around waiting for the day that He would be killed on that cross and think "well I'm going to die, so who really cares how I live anyway." No! He made waves. Big ones. He helped people, He healed people, He disturbed the ways of the world. Yes, He knew He would be killed anyway, but He lived with God right by His side. He knocked mountains down and caused earthquakes. We need to live as Jesus did. He didn't let this world distract from the plan that God had. He ran into that plan, head first. Without God's direction, Jesus would have just been a normal guy. But with God, Jesus made sure that you and I would have a world with the Holy Spirit flowing through us. A way to connect to God's wisdom, and a way to move mountains to show others that their mountains can be moved as well.

Charles Stanly said, "As you walk through the valley of the unknown, you will find the footprints of Jesus both in front of you and beside you." It's kind of cool right? No matter where you walk, He is right there with you. Just because you can't see Him there, doesn't mean He isn't. You can't see your own brain either, but you still use it and believe it's there. Imagine if you just started to doubt that you have a brain to use. It wouldn't get you very far in life now, would it? The same goes for being with God. Once you kick Him out or push His hand away from you, it's really hard to get far on your own. So don't do it. Take a step back and make sure you really are walking with God. It can be easy to forget that He's there with you. It can seem like the whole world is caving in on you because of how you are following His plan. I started listening to everyone else around me instead of listening to the one who lives in me. It didn't get me far. It got me really messed up, really quick.

I want to challenge you to something right now. I had to make a hard decision, and it's one that I want you to commit to making right now. Starting at this moment, make a vow to listen to God. Not to your sister, your mother, your best friend, your brother, or anyone else. Usually, God wants to take you somewhere completely unexpected and out of your comfort zone. Your friends and family don't know what God knows, so they are only coming from a place that is either filled with worry, fear, or something else deep inside of them that would not make the choices that you have to make right now. Most people walk by sight, not by faith, but as Christians, we are taught that we have to rely completely on our faith, and not by what we see. God's ways aren't usually conventional, but they are always worth it.

Here is a little bit of my personal story at this moment in time. Like I've said before, I'm writing this book while I'm going through this trial in my life. I don't want to wait for it to all be done before I take you through it. I want this to be real, raw, honest, and really show you how God is moving in my life. Everything currently in my life is pointing to a broken marriage. It's officially been nine months since we separated, and the outlook...well, there really isn't one. There is nothing that I can see that shows me that my marriage will ever be whole or repaired ever again. That's the whole point in walking by faith and not sight. I can't see an outcome that is good. Luckily for me, I don't have to see it.

Last week I spoke to a Pastor about being stuck. I felt like I was just going through the motions and nothing was changing. It didn't look like my husband was changing, wanting to change, or as anything had even shifted in his world. I had just kept going back and forth with "should I stay with him, and wait for him, or should I get divorce papers ready?" I never made a choice, I just kept floating. I felt like I was losing my mind, and I really wasn't clear on what God wanted me to do. After I told her this, she prayed with me but then this is what her advice was this:

"Ok, Shannon, this is what I'm going to tell you to do. You have to make a choice. You can't just expect God to make the choice for you and give you all the answers. Just like Paul, he took a step and God would give him peace when he was going in the right direction. If he didn't have peace, he'd take a step back and go in another direction, until he felt that unwavering peace from the Lord. So you are going to have to make a decision. Don't make it based on what anyone else says. Make it according to what you truly believe God wants you to do. Once you make that choice, whether it's to stay with him, or divorce him, make an effort to walk towards that and actively do something about it. You will know by the peace that God does or doesn't give you if you're on the right track. If you start going towards your decision and it immediately feels wrong, then back up and go the other way. God will guide you. But you have to make a choice."

I needed this so bad because I felt like my mind was playing ping pong. So I prayed and fasted, then I made a choice. I made the choice to take divorce off of the table completely. I also made the choice to not talk about it to anyone. Once you start telling people what you think God is leading you to do, you will be flooded with opinions. Some right, most wrong. I know that right now if I told any of my friends this choice, they'd all tell me I'm crazy, or maybe even stupid. The thing is, they're looking at this situation by sight, not by faith. Once I made this choice, I started actively going towards it, meaning no distractions, no dating, no talking bad about him, praying for him daily with intention, fasting, and really praying for true change in my husband. Having endurance in my faith, I became overwhelmed with peace. I don't know if this is your path, don't follow my choice. You need to make your own, but you need to make the right one. Let God show you peace, or take you another way if you aren't feeling that peace. God's plan for your life will be different from mine. You may be meant for the same thing, or something else. The whole point is to rely on Him. Don't let your own fears stand between you and God. You're nothing without Him. If you asked yourself if you were better off with or without God, I can promise that the answer is with Him. I want you to keep this verse in mind, "No eye has seen, no ear has heard, no mind has imagined what God has prepared for those who love Him." (1 Corinthians 2:9 NLT)

nine

When I was a kid I would go to places with my Grandma that sold Fool's Gold and I used to think it was so cool. She didn't, and I didn't understand why. I looked at that little golden nugget and basically saw my way into a rich life. I was also like eight years old, and hadn't quite put together its name, that very literally told you it wasn't real gold. That's how we are as humans, sometimes we see this shiny little thing and we think it's something that it's not. If you've never heard of The Golden Nugget or Fool's Gold, basically it's a yellow mineral that looks like actual gold to the untrained eye. It's cheap and you can pretty much buy it at any place that you can take a field trip to, that tells you about all the old times with cowboys. Honestly, most truck stops have them as little souvenirs too. Or at least they did when I was younger, I haven't really looked into it much since then.

My point is that it is very common, super cheap, and pretends to be something that it isn't. That is why I'm naming this chapter after it. Honestly, this chapter isn't one that I'm proud to write, nor did I look forward to it. I've known that I was going to write about this from the beginning, because it's something that came into my life so fast after my husband left, and I didn't realize it until it hurt me. So here is my warning to you. Beware of that sneaky little nugget, it'll come for you when you are at your lowest, and you'll never see it coming unless you're expecting it.

Now obviously I don't mean an actual nugget of fool's gold. It's more of a metaphor if you will. Your weakness, your Achilles heel, your kryptonite. That is what a golden nugget is, and it is very specific to YOU. Everyone has one, you could have more than one, but you definitely have one. This is the thing that the devil uses to trip you up. It could be anything from drinking, to porn, to flirting, to anxiety or depression, even guilt. If for whatever reason you don't know what yours is, although I'm betting as you read this your mind just went somewhere and you know exactly what I mean, find out quickly because it will be used against you. To help you out a bit I'm going to talk about mine, even though this may be the hardest thing to talk about. It is my weakness after all, and honestly, I'm still trying to navigate through it as best as I can. I'm sort of hoping this will help me out in a way as well because I've been dreading this part of the book. Once it's out there, well you know the rest.

Moving on. I've always had abandonment issues for as long as I can remember. My biological father wasn't ever really in the picture, because he chose a life of drug and alcohol abuse over me. My stepdad, who is pretty great now, used to have an alcohol problem and was a workaholic so he wasn't really ever around much either. As I grew up I found that I had this obsession with having a boyfriend. As a kid, I guess you just say that someone is boy-crazy. But in all seriousness I constantly had a boyfriend, I was terrified to be alone, I didn't like it. I loved the idea of holding someone's hand or going to the movies or a park, or the mall, honestly anywhere as long as I wasn't alone. Now sure I had tons of friends but it wasn't the same. It was like I was searching to be wanted by a guy because obviously, I had daddy issues, I just didn't know it at the time. The more I grew up and grew into the person I was meant to be, the faster I started losing more men. My uncles stopped talking to me, cousins would leave and just lose connection, and as for the guys that I liked, well that was a whole other battle in itself.

I honestly can't tell you a time during school when I was actually single. Please bear in mind that I don't mean I was out sleeping with everyone. I know that some people think that is what not being single means. I just wanted someone to call my boyfriend. It made me feel like someone was there forever, and would never leave. Even if they were only my boyfriend for a week. I'm talking super young here guys. I remember my first boyfriend, I was in kindergarten. KINDERGARTEN. If you ask my mom it was just a cute little crush I had. In my eyes, he was my first kiss, my first crush, my first best friend, and that lasted through like fourth grade. My family and his family knew each other, we had sleepovers, and our brothers played together. Weird? Yea, maybe. But for me, even at such a young age, it was stability. It was a man in my life that wasn't leaving like my dad did. It was a boy choosing me on purpose. And that was just the beginning my friends.

When I moved schools after sixth grade it got worse. I fell for a twin. I was obsessed with this guy. He treated me terribly, constantly ignored me, and barely did anything that even remotely showed that he was my boyfriend. Yet somehow people knew we were together. We constantly broke up and got back together for about two and a half years. It was sad and man do I wish I could go back and shake my tween self. He wasn't really that cute, and the fact that he really didn't seem to care if I was with him or not should have bothered me more than it actually did. The summer before high school I ended up dating this guy from Mexico. Yes, ladies, a boy in another country. Mind you, I had met him in person while visiting my grandma (my stepdad is Mexican and we used to go down there every summer to visit family). For whatever stupid reason, we thought that a long-distance relationship would work, until I found out that he really didn't seem to care much about me. My cousins from Mexico would call and tell me they saw him out and about with other girls and it broke my heart. Yet I still felt like I needed him. A boy who didn't really want me unless it was convenient for him.

A little into freshman year we ended things, because I just couldn't handle it anymore. He was too far away and I didn't trust him. Plus there was a sea of fresh teen boys at my High School. Ok, pause for just a second. I realize as I'm reading over this that I sound like a total creep. Or like a lioness waiting to pounce. I assure you that wasn't the case. In all reality, I just wanted to be wanted. I wanted a boy to choose me because he wanted to, not because I gave him an ultimatum. I was searching for love, real love, and validation, from dumb teenage boys. It didn't help that I was 14 and completely clueless. I'm sure some of you have been there. Or maybe I'm totally alone on this, but I have to explain all of this before I can go into detail about my golden nugget situation.

So anyway, back to High School. Entering my sophomore year, I met a boy that changed my life. He taught me what love was. As much as I had said those words to almost every other boy I had been with, I really meant it with this one. I felt it with him. This was my first serious relationship. We talked about everything from the future to religion and politics (which neither of us really knew about because we were so young) and anything else in between. The other thing that was different about this guy, was that he had me in such a trance that I threw most of my morals out the window. I didn't want him going anywhere and I truly believed I knew what love was.

Growing up, I had always had the plan to save myself for marriage. My friends knew that the guys I had dated knew that, and my best guy friend, Alfred, also knew that. Being so young, it was easy to think I knew what was right for myself. Alfred was the only one really keeping me in line. Reminding me who I was and what I valued. He was the one reminding me that I wanted to wait until marriage, that I was a good girl, a God girl. He didn't like my boyfriend because he could see right through him. I guess being a guy, he knew exactly how he thought. He tried warning me and I ignored him. Then I ended up losing my virginity a few months after turning 16.

Now by no means was Alfred a saint. Not even in the slightest. But he respected my boundaries, my beliefs, and who I was and wanted to be. Something that my boyfriend at the time didn't care much about. He tried to remain that little voice in my head telling me not to go swim in the deep end, but I let the golden nugget dangle. Why? Well, probably because I was so young, but also because I wanted what I didn't have and I wanted it now. I didn't want to wait on God to move. I figured this was the best thing in the world for me and I'd never had it better. Do you follow where I'm headed with this?

For the next few years, all of my girlfriends cheered us on and loved our relationship. So I thought anyway. Alfred was still very vocal about how he disliked my boyfriend, but I still didn't listen. We ended up getting engaged my senior year, which felt normal and right to me. He was already out of High School and in the military, so we had our wedding date set for August of 2010. I had my dream dress picked out and the only future plans I had was to be a military wife and go wherever he had to go.

Then in May of 2010, he came home from a three-month training in California, and straight-up told me "I don't want to get married, I don't love you anymore." Not only was I in shock, but my future was about to explode right in my face. I was a 19-year-old hairdresser who had no other future plans than to be a wife and shove out a bunch of kids. I didn't want to be a hairdresser forever. If I'm being honest, I really only did it because I was good at it and I could work on any US military base with my license. I didn't understand how my life was literally falling apart. Shortly after we broke up I found out that all of my friends hated him, they just never spoke up. They didn't like how he had changed me and he was no good for me. This was serious news to me because I didn't know that anyone disliked him. If I would have paid attention to how everyone acted around him, then I would have known how they felt. I didn't know I had changed for the worse. Yet there was Alfred, fully behind me, ready to tackle my now ex-fiance. He didn't rub it in my face, he didn't say "I told you so" and he didn't make me feel dumber than I already felt. He knew all along that this guy was not the one for me, but he stood by my side and let me go through what I needed to go through to find the truth. The reason I'm even telling this story is that I want you to see how God really is with us. We make stupid choices, He'll tell us how He feels, and then it's up to us how to navigate our lives. Even if we decided to take our lives in our own direction and not His, He is still going to be there walking right by your side through the whole thing. The moment that it all blows up in your face, which most likely it will at some point, God is right there waiting to give you a hug, pick you up, and help you get back to the original direction that you should have gone down in the first place.

This was well over 10 years ago, but it's a vital part of my life story. You'll see why here in a bit. After we broke up, I had to make the choice to keep my wedding dress, this beautiful Cinderella dream dress, or basically give it back to the bridal shop and lose our deposit, which was 50% of the cost of the dress. I came to the conclusion, after a long talk with my parents, that it was better to give the dress back to the shop. If I was ever to marry someone I didn't want the same dress I had to marry someone else in. Plus it would only bring me painful memories of our entire relationship.

Once all of the wedding plans were canceled, I began to spiral. Instead of running to God, I ran everywhere else. I kept asking "Why God? Why me? Why did you let him leave?" Stupid questions really, because God obviously had so much better for me than what I had for me. I wish I had known that at the time, but instead I began a long journey of spiraling out of control. I started drinking to forget him, then I started partying and clubbing trying to have fun and find myself again. I went on date after date with guys who were all wrong for me because I just wanted to be loved. I started messing around with guys with whom I had no business being around. Older guys, brothers of some friends, the "bad-boys" from high school, even a friend of an uncle. I would literally show up to the church at times hungover. It was the worst time of my life and I felt like I was going through it all alone. All I wanted was someone to reach out and guide me in the right direction but I didn't want to ask for help, I didn't want to be told I was wrong or messy or that I needed God in my life to help me fix it. I was a disaster on the inside that looked great on the outside.

I spiraled weekly for almost a year until I finally decided to calm down. I realized that what I was wanting and looking for, I wasn't finding. I remember one friend telling me something that really stuck with me. She said "I was looking for someone for so long. Telling God exactly what I wanted in a man. Then one day I realized that I needed to stop praying that God brings me the man I want, and to lead me to the man that He wants and I need." I had never heard anyone put it like that and I was blown away. In all honesty, I didn't even know what kind of guy I wanted. I just didn't want to be alone, and that just brought any and every guy into the picture. Then I let go of trying to force myself into meeting someone. I stopped trying to date and I stopped chasing guys. That is when I met my husband.

See, the enemy knows what your weakness is. He knows what you really want and he uses that to his advantage to get you sidetracked. He's smart and swift, so we have to be smarter. Usually, that means we have to follow what God is telling us to do because most of the time, we do what we want, not what He wants. God knows what we actually need, even if it may not be what we want at the time. But girl, let me just tell you that God's not surprised by what you do. He knew you were going to spiral, He knew you were going to go after your best friend's brother. He stuck by you anyway, because you needed to be taught a lesson. You basically have two choices, listen to what God tells you to do, or learn a huge lesson by doing the opposite.

Fast forward to my husband walking out on me. I felt like I was repeating history. I was so wrecked I didn't know what to do or how to feel or what to think. I was lost and stuck. I let my guard down and guess what?! The devil took his little opportunity to jump right in with my golden nugget. I'll say it again and again, your weakness will be your nugget, okay. Be it drinking, gambling, love, anxiety, depression, etc. He'll use whatever he can to throw you off course and make your life a mess. He's slick, and if you let your guard down, you won't even see it coming, until it's too late. Although I'm hoping that this book, this chapter, and telling you this will help you see it earlier.

Now on to my golden nugget. I was a disaster when all of this went down, as you've read in some previous chapters. Part of me wanted to spiral like I did when I got dumped a few months before my wedding with my previous ex. I was a different person then and I wasn't strong in my faith. I wasn't strong mentally at all if I'm being honest. Frankly, I felt like I was too old to spiral, even though I've seen people way older than me out of control, I just felt like it wouldn't do me any good.

Side note: Now look, I decided to write this book knowing full well that some people I know may read it and I'm not proud of most of this, but I've always thought that it's better to be transparent than to let people think that I'm perfect. NO ONE IS PERFECT. Yes, I'm screaming this at you because you shouldn't feel like you have to be, or like you have to pretend you are. So it would be stupid of you to think that I'm supposed to be a perfect Christian. I'm not. I'm learning and growing each day. This isn't to excuse anything I've done, but to let you know that you're going to mess up sometimes and it's ok. God sees your heart, He knows what's going on with you, with me, and with Bonnie down the street. Just do your best, even if your best kind of sucks sometimes.

So anyway, back to him leaving me. I did ok for about a month or so. I think it was because I just thought it was a fight that would blow over soon. Until it didn't. Then I started to let fear creep in. Then one day I just couldn't handle it anymore. I was so upset, so mad and hurt that I decided I'd drink. Now keep in mind that I hadn't really drank anything at all since I was 21, and here we are almost 10 years later and I thought it would be a great idea. Spoiler, it wasn't, but I did it anyway. I went to a friend's place and drank one, yes ONE drink. One drink almost knocked me out. True story, I'm a lightweight. That night didn't go how I wanted and I felt absolutely terrible the next morning and I woke up thinking "Really Shannon? This is what we've come to?" I knew it wasn't for me. Since then I drank two more times and then decided I was done. There's no point to it, and it just makes me feel like I'm dying. Thanks but no thanks.

Remember how I said the enemy will sneak in with what he knows will take you out? Well, he quickly realized it wouldn't be drinking. But man did he find a way in. It was with another guy. This truly hit me out of nowhere. I wasn't looking for anyone, plus I was still married. I didn't know what was going to happen but at the same time, I felt so beyond alone that it was hard to sleep at night. This person was someone who I never even looked at that way until he started hitting on me more and more. Ok so another side note, when you're with someone for so long, and someone flirts with you, sometimes you miss it. It took a minute for me to catch on to what this guy was doing. I even asked some friends if this was flirting and they agreed it was.

 I didn't see the harm in it since I was basically going to be a single mom. I figured my marriage was over, my husband left me, and I'm not doing anything wrong because we're just talking. I've known this guy for quite some time and he was always the sweetest person to me. So when I started to notice that he had actually been flirting with me for months, I was kind of shocked. He knew my situation and everything I was going through. He had talked to me about it because he was in a weird relationship with someone else who wasn't really on the same page as him so I honestly liked talking to him about this mess. We're going to call him Chandler for safety measures. So Chandler started flirting and talking to me a lot, but then he pulled back because he had tried to rekindle the relationship that he told me about. Well, then things ended with him and her and we talked more and more. He was giving me so much attention but also being super sweet, nice, and funny. Truth be told, it was just a nice change of pace because it took my mind off of everything. Queue scene for the enemy to sneak in his little plan. I started thinking about this guy, Chandler, non-stop. It was kind of ridiculous. But I felt like I was 15 crushing on someone. You know, the butterflies and whatnot.

 This was a whole new world for me. I didn't know what I was feeling and I didn't know what he was feeling. But I liked it. I was so scared that I'd never find anyone after my husband. I didn't think there was any possible way for me to feel something for someone else because I was so in love with the man I married. So this thing with Chandler helped me realize that I could feel again. Now hear me out, I wasn't looking for love or even a boyfriend. I didn't even want to go on a date with this guy, but the attention and the way he made me smile was more than what I could have asked for. Until it blew up in my face one night.

If I would have known asking for a simple favor from him would have ended the way it did, I never would have texted him in the first place. We ended up talking all day long. Sure it was a little flirty but it truly seemed like an innocent conversation between the two of us. The more we talked the quicker it went from just flirting to something very intimate and unexpected. I let my guard down with him and he fully carried the conversation right into something out of 50 Shades of Grey (I haven't read that book, let alone seen the movie but I know what it's about). Chandler was very smooth with his words. He knew how to talk to me, and he knew how to get me to talk to him how he wanted. As the night went on, it only got more intense, and he made his official move on me. Up until this point, it had been five months without my husband. Five months without sex. Yup. We're about to get very honest right here. It's hard for me to talk about sex so easily, but I feel like if we don't talk about it, or at least bring it up a little bit in this book, it'll seem like it's not important. But it is. Especially being a Christian.

Chandler put up an offer on the table that was very hard for me to pass up, but thankfully I was strong enough to turn him down. It would have been so easy to let him come over so late at night. Everyone was asleep, no one would know besides us, and my husband already left me and who knows when I'd ever sleep with anyone else again. I was trying so hard to justify it. I was lonely and this guy wanted me. I wanted to say yes. I wanted to feel someone holding me, I wanted to feel something again. For months I had just felt numb. He tried so hard to persuade me by saying "I'm right down the street from your house, I can just come over, no one would know." I finally forced the answer out of my mouth and said "No, I can't. I want to, but I'm not in the place mentally for it." He let it go and said ok I'll talk to you tomorrow, go to bed. I really thought that was the end of it. I thought I got out free and clear. I went to bed.

About 30 minutes later around 3 am, I heard my phone buzzing. He woke me up just to tell me he got home safe and sound. I congratulated him and tried to go back to bed but he kept texting me. Flirty texts, one after another until texts weren't enough. Then he started sending pictures. Pictures that I didn't ask for, and on any other occasion would have made me block him. Not on this night. No, this night I fed into it, I fell right into the devils trap and I sent pictures back. Our conversation and pictures went back and forth until about 5 am. The whole thing escalated so quickly that it took me by surprise and by the time I woke up the next morning I had no clue what had just happened.

I ended up getting way too much into my feelings, thinking that this guy actually liked me only to end up hurt and living with the regret of that night. Honest to God I still don't fully get what happened but all of a sudden he started ignoring me and acting like he never even spoke to me in the first place. At first, I was thinking maybe it was weird for him since he was fresh out of a relationship, but then I started thinking with insecurities. I started to question myself. Maybe I'm too overweight, too short, maybe it's because I have two kids or baby daddy drama. Maybe I'm too weird or goofy or I came on too strong. I would literally think to myself "of course there couldn't be anything wrong with him, only me, I mean my husband did leave me, not the other way around. So I must be the problem." First of all, NO! I wish I could turn back time and give myself a good slap. The devil wants to put all these insecurities and bad thoughts into your head and flip your world upside down. If God says you are worthy, then YOU ARE WORTHY!! It doesn't matter what anyone else thinks, only what God says. What you did doesn't matter, because He redeemed you. Sometimes it's just hard for us to remember that. Regardless, Chandler started ignoring me hard, unless he needed something from me of course. Then I ended up finding out a bunch of things about him that showed me how terrible he really was. I felt so used and taken advantage of and it hurt me. Now I can sit here all day long and say "Well IF I just ignored him, to begin with, I wouldn't be in this situation. I wouldn't be feeling hurt." Sure that's probably true, but I also wouldn't have learned this lesson. I wouldn't have learned that I needed to seek out what God wanted for me instead of letting this Golden Nugget dangle in front of me.

The enemy used bait, and I took it. You know it's kind of funny, I always heard people use the saying "Shoulda Coulda Woulda" and I didn't even get it so I modified it to make sense to me "Shoulda Coulda Didn't". Ok sounds crazy I know but hear me out. I SHOULD HAVE ignored him. I COULD HAVE ignored him. I DIDN'T ignore him. Those are the facts. This man-made me go against my better judgment and throw out my morals. I regret letting him trick me but I learned from it. A mistake is only a failure if you didn't learn anything from it.

I'm hoping you don't have to go through anything like this, but there is a big chance that you will. As women, we tend to do everything based on our emotions. It's stupid, but it's true. Sometimes it works out for us in a great way, other times it ruins us. I've just learned that with all the mess-ups, all the mistakes, and all the sleepless nights thinking about how I could have done things differently, there is hope. Hope that if you can learn from this situation, you'll be quicker to fight off the enemy with the next thing he dangles in front of you. You can only get smarter from here. So if there is something that you're thinking of right now that you think knocked you off track. Something you did that makes you wonder if God is looking down on you thinking "Wow you're a hot mess, I'm not gonna help you out anymore". Whatever that thing is, just chat with the Big Man about it. One amazing thing about God is that He is unbelievably understanding. When Jesus was down here walking around, He had so much compassion for people. People who were a real mess; criminals, adulterers, and some people who just didn't get it, yet He had compassion on them. He still forgave them, loved them, and pointed them in the right direction.

God seriously loves you so much, even if you fell for your golden nugget and He isn't going to hold it against you. I mean I personally believe that this had to happen to make me stronger, wiser and to help you with it if you're going through it now. Get this, in 2 Chronicles 36:15 it says "The Lord, the God of their ancestors, repeatedly sent his prophets to warn them, for he had compassion on his people and his Temple." How cool is that? He sent warnings REPEATEDLY. The definition of repeatedly is over and over again; constantly. God has so much compassion, He won't just warn or help you once or twice. But over and over and over again until you get it right. I mean that's pretty neat in my book. Someone has to really love you to not give up on you but to go after you repeatedly. So if you messed up, or if you do tomorrow, and you fall into this dumb trap that the enemy is laying out for you, don't feel like a failure. Pick yourself up, acknowledge your personalized nugget of gold, Fool's Gold rather, and dust yourself off and keep heading towards the direction that God is sending you in. He won't quit on you, so don't quit on yourself. Once the devil realizes that you aren't one to give up, he'll quickly see that you're not going to go down without a huge fight. I'm not saying he'll back off, but things will get easier as you go because you're getting stronger in your faith walk.

Sometimes, quotes and scriptures help you feel a bit more at ease, so I have a few that will hopefully help you remember who your God is, and how amazing He is.

- The righteous person faces many troubles, but the Lord comes to the rescue each time. For the Lord protects the bones of the righteous; not one of them is broken! (Psalms 34:19-20 NLT)
- But in that coming day, no weapon turned against you will succeed. You will silence every voice raised up to accuse you. These benefits are enjoyed by the servants of the Lord; their vindication will come from me. I, the Lord, have spoken! (Isaiah 54:17 NLT)
- The devil doesn't know what to do with somebody who just won't give up. -Joyce Meyer
- She questioned her own worth, at times, because of the scars she had picked up along the journey. But then she heard God whisper "You are mine, The Daughter of the King. Don't forget who you are." -Tracy Hagler
- But as for you, be strong and courageous, for your work will be rewarded. (2 Corinthians 15:7 NLT)

ten

I really wanted to dedicate a full chapter to prayer and fasting. These are the things that are going to give you results, answers, guidance, strength and so much more. Maybe this is obvious to some of you. Maybe it's not. As someone who has been going to a full gospel, tongue talking, praise, and worshiping church since I was about 11, these are things we've always been taught. Pray about everything and fast often. I heard these things all the time. But when your marriage, and life in general, starts going south really fast, you may forget what you were taught.

I've been praying since I was a little girl before I ever got saved. It's something that my mom had taught me at a young age. We didn't grow up going to church or Sunday school. We really only even stepped into a church if someone was getting married. So it's not something I did often, and I didn't memorize prayers. I didn't know the prayer that people said right before they ate and I definitely didn't know hymns. But If I was scared or happy, I just talked to God. I remember at a really young age, my mom said that these people kept coming to our door, very often and harassing her. She said that she prayed and asked God to make them stop and they never came back. That has literally stuck with me my entire life. When I heard that, I'm pretty sure that was the moment my faith started. She asked God to help, and He did. That was all I needed to know. I remember praying for things at school, with friends, family matters, things that scared me, things I wanted, etc. I just talked to God. I don't ever remember there being a moment that I didn't believe that He'd answer my prayers. I always knew that He would hear me, no matter what.

So, I invite you to start praying like that if you aren't already. Pray with intention. Pray about what you need, where you should go, what you should do, how to overcome this, or anything else that comes your way. In your head, out loud, in a journal, however you want to talk to God, just do it. That's really all prayer is. Just a conversation with the coolest dude in the world. Yea I get that it sounds a bit corny, but just because something sounds simple, docsn't mean it's not effective. Let me be the first to tell you that it's beyond effective. "Don't worry about anything; instead, pray about everything. Tell God what you need, and thank him for all he has done." (Philippians 4:6 NLT)

I mean how cool is that? God wants you to ask Him for what you need. He wants to talk to you. He wants to hear about your day, and what you have going on in your head. He cares that much. You can't annoy him. It's nuts right?! I know there are a lot of people I have annoyed and I know that I definitely get annoyed sometimes. But God, never. He is so happy when you come to Him. It's what He wants. He looks forward to it. He even answers you back. So not only can you tell Him every little thing on your mind and not pay Him $100 an hour, but He also meets you where you are and gives you answers. You may not hear His voice in your ear, but you'll know it in your heart when He answers. "In those days when you pray, I will listen." (Jeremiah 29:12 NLT)

We serve an amazing God. A God who cares about our feelings, our marriage, and even getting a good parking spot. Maybe you know this already. Maybe you pray daily and you wake up thanking The Lord for another day of life. I know I did. I prayed a lot. I prayed when I was sad when I was happy, grumpy, irritated, complaining, and grateful. I honestly bugged Him throughout the entire day. I have no shame about it. I love talking to God, It really came naturally to me.

That is until my husband left and I was angry. My prayers started out flustered. You know what I mean "God make him say sorry" or "God why did he do this, he needs to fix this" or even "God what am I supposed to do now? I'm lost and confused, and angry at him. Why did he ruin our family?". Yup, I used all of those. Then I came across a reading plan on my bible app about praying for my husband. Wouldn't you know, I was doing it all wrong. I needed to stop trying to force what I wanted to happen with my husband, and start praying with intention. I needed to start praying specific prayers that were going to really change things. That's what prayer does, it moves mountains, and breaks down prison walls. And I'm over here using it to try and get sympathy or make my husband feel bad for what he did. All the while, he's already beating himself, and I'm trying to pour gasoline on his already burning fire.

I needed to get specific and consistent with what I was really praying for. I also needed to remember that when the time comes that I don't feel like praying for him, because trust me those days will indeed come, I needed to have the discipline to pray no matter what I felt. Why? Because when the devil sees you giving up, that's when he starts to move in. When you stay consistent and intentional, you basically form a bubble of protection around you, your husband, and your marriage. Trust me, you'll need that bubble. Because while you're praying your little heart out, every attack possible is going to come at him. You may never know what he has gone, or is going through. Just seeing my husband's face on the phone when he talks to the kids every once and a while, I know for a fact that the devil realized that he couldn't stop me so he went after him full force. The enemy will come mentally, physically, and spiritually. He looks for the weak spots and rips them open until there is nothing left. Only one problem with that, your husband married YOU! A woman of faith. A woman who is doing everything in her power to not be like the world and walk away from her marriage. A woman that gets up in the morning and dresses in the full armor of God and is ready for battle. Drinking her coffee and saying "Not Today Satan!", with a strong stern voice and belief to back it up. Yea he took one look at you and knew he couldn't mess with you, he couldn't distract you, so he went after your husband.

Now look, I know how this starts off so there's no fooling me. You of course want to pray for him. You want things to change, you want to witness those mountain-moving miracles that you know God can do. You feel something else is meant for you and your marriage. Something huge. So you keep praying. One month goes by and you are still going strong. Then four months go by and you don't see anything happening, but you still pray. Eight months are creeping past you and you're tired. You don't want to pray for him anymore. It's not like he's over there praying for you. He doesn't care if you pray for him. Maybe it's time to move on. Maybe it's time to just give up. I mean you don't see anything changing at all. You haven't gotten any answers. What's the point? Well if it isn't obvious already, the point is things WILL change, because they HAVE to change.

Praying and not believing what you are praying for is beyond pointless. So if you're just saying these prayers and not believing that God is going to do what you are asking for, you may not see many results. Belief is a massive part of prayer. Jesus said "I tell you, you can pray for anything, and if you believe that you've received it, it will be given to you." (Mark 11:24 NLT) Now don't get dumb, if you ask God to run your husband over, He's not going to do that. Your prayers need to be within reason, but If you're asking God to bring him back home, to change and restore your marriage, then why wouldn't He do that for you?

In Luke 18 Jesus tells his disciples a story to prove to them that prayer works. He told them that they should ALWAYS pray and NEVER give up (Luke 18:1 NLT) Why would Jesus tell you to never give up? Maybe he didn't understand how hard it would be to pray for a man who hurt you. Maybe Jesus just had no clue that praying just wasn't going to work on your husband. He forgot it only worked sometimes. Or maybe he's just up there in Heaven ignoring you.

Seriously if any of these are your thoughts just stop right now. None of that is even remotely true. God hears everything you say. He's working on it, you just don't see it yet. Remember, He's never early and never late, He's always right on time. "God has made everything beautiful for its own time. He has planted eternity in the human heart, but even so, people can't see the whole scope of God's work from beginning to end." (Ecclesiastes 3:11 NLT)

In Luke, Jesus starts talking about this woman who went to a judge. The judge didn't care about God and he really didn't care about people. Who knows, maybe he was just in it for the money or maybe even the power. But this woman kept coming to him demanding justice for what had happened to her. This woman did what we all do best and annoyed this man until he finally caved. He literally said "this woman is driving me crazy. I'm going to see that she gets justice…" (Luke 18:5 NLT) He wasn't even a believer but he gave her what she wanted because she was so persistent and didn't stop asking. Jesus went on to say that even if a judge who wasn't a God-fearing man, and didn't care about people gave her justice, wouldn't God give it to his own people who cry out to him? Yes. Yes, He would, and He will.

I've made sure that through all of this I remember that. I remember to ask and seek diligently. I bug God non-stop. For months I've been praying that God will show me what it is I'm supposed to do. Should I wait for my husband? Should I walk away and divorce him? I've also been very specifically praying that my husband will have a "Saul to Paul transformation". You don't have to pray those exact words. But that is what was on my heart. My thinking was "Ok God you took this terrible man who hated Jesus and killed a ton of Christians, and you took him and used him to write a lot of the Bible, and go all over the place and heal people, get them saved, and literally talk about Jesus everywhere he went. If you can do that with a horrible person like Saul, I KNOW that you CAN do it for my husband." I've been praying those same words, over and over again. "God, give him a Saul to Paul transformation!" And guess what?! I didn't tell anyone that I was praying those specific words either. Not because I didn't want anyone to know, but because I wanted to make sure that if God was going to answer me, I'd know it was God. Make sense?

I ended up going to a women's conference in Oklahoma, and before I left on a 6-hour road trip with some friends I prayed one more time. I knew this was going to be a life-changing event. I went EXPECTING to be guided by God. I EXPECTED to get answers. Even if they were answers that I didn't want.

So I prayed "I'm going to this thing, and I'm open. I'm going to stay open and whatever I get from there I'm going to run with it. But I'm also going to get answers. God, if what you want me to do is to stay in place, and wait for my husband to come home, I need to know that he WILL have a Saul to Paul transformation. If not, if you want me to walk away, Let them preach or talk about something that has to do with Boaz. So that I know I'll find another. That you'll take care of me and my kids and I will be ok."

When you expect God to answer your prayers, He will. It may be through a dream, a sermon, a person, or a song. He may even guide you to a specific passage while you're reading your Bible. He WILL answer you, you just have to listen. Once I got to this conference, I was already so at peace. The first service started and I was excited. Immediately the Pastor started talking about Paul. How much she liked him, how great he was, what he had gone through, and so on. But, being the stubborn person I am, I just chalked that up to a coincidence. There was no way I could get my answer on the first night, right?! It amazes me how patient God is with us.

The next morning, another Preacher started talking about Paul, again I was stubborn. Inside I thought, "Well she didn't say the EXACT words I had been praying so I still don't have my answer." Wow! Just wow. Look I'm just gonna say this, if you ask God for something, don't be so stubborn to listen when He answers. Following that service, there was about a 30-minute break. Once the next Preacher got up there, she immediately started talking about Paul. As if they had all planned this, which by the way they hadn't even talked about their messages. I almost rolled my eyes, but God knows me too well. Within minutes she said word for word "Paul is a great guy, but he wasn't always, he had to have the SAUL TO PAUL TRANSFORMATION." I almost fell out of the pew. Ok God, I finally got it. I could feel the tears accumulating inside of me. I knew this was my answer. I finally knew that the "feeling" that I had been getting about not divorcing my husband was what God was telling me. What's even better, is God knows what is going to throw us off course.

Remember how I said that I prayed if I should walk away, that I need to hear about Boaz? Well, we were only on day 2, so I got nervous. What if someone preaches on that? Then what? Then what do I do? Sure enough the next day someone started teaching and talking about Ruth. I was terrified. Not terrified that I needed to walk away, but that I'd be more confused about what to do. Well, nothing surprises God. He led me to go to this conference for a reason. He knew what these women would teach, what they would say and not say. Guess what? Boaz was NEVER mentioned. Not once. Man did God know me. He knew I'd freak out and get confused if I heard that name. So He made sure that I didn't.

God knows what we need, and he hears every single prayer that we have. He'll answer you, especially when you continue to pray that HIS WILL BE DONE and not yours. I learned that I have to surrender to what God wants and once I do that, He'll take care of the rest. Now look I was so happy that I got my answer but that didn't mean I wasn't still a bit worried. It doesn't really look like my husband is coming home, or even wants to. Honestly, the way that it looks right at this moment, I'm never getting him back. Thank goodness I'm a child of God, that means I walk by faith NOT by sight. Meaning that no matter what things look like on the outside, my job is to have the faith to trust that God is going to do what He promised. Is it hard to walk by faith? Absolutely. Will it be worth it? Most definitely. It's always hard while you're walking through it. That's exactly why you need to have a prayer routine. Be intentional, be specific, and believe what you are praying for.

Now for step number two, fasting. Fasting isn't as practiced or as talked about as prayer. I feel like everyone always talks about praying and talking to God. It's a great habit to get into and it'll get you answers and results. Definitely pray, and don't stop, but start incorporating fasting into your prayer life as well. If you don't know what fasting is, or maybe you do but you've never done it, or maybe haven't done it often, it's pretty simple. The short version; basically you are sacrificing something important to you and giving it up to be closer to God. Usually, fasting involves giving up or reducing certain foods. I've fasted for 3 days with only liquids. I've done the Daniel fast which is basically only having fruits and veggies. That wasn't always the case though. When I first started to fast, I knew that if I was giving up something that mattered to me, then God would know where I was coming from and He would still answer me. I was really praying for something a few years back and I really thought that I knew what the answer was. But I wanted to be on the safe side, so I decided to give up any and all music that didn't glorify God. Now I don't listen to trashy music, but I love coffee house music and sometimes love songs, some good 'ole Frank Sinatra is always a favorite. But I decided to only listen to Christian and gospel music until I got my answer. Not only did doing this get the answer that I needed, but it also made my relationship with God so much better. I had more peace, clarity, and faith.

Please, do not think that fasting is easy. The whole point of it is to surrender the desires of your flesh. If the enemy can get you to not pay attention to the Holy Spirit, then he'll knock you off track and it's a win for him. If you can keep your flesh, or worldly desires for lack of better words, under control then you'll have so much insight into the Kingdom of God.

Earlier this year one of my friends recommended that I read the book The hidden power of prayer & fasting by Mahesh Chavda. This book gave me so much insight into how to pray and fast the correct and most effective way. He really teaches about fasting in a way that is easy to understand. In this book, Mahesh talks about the 9 reasons we fast, so I'm going to list them out to you, just in case you don't go get this book. Though I definitely recommend that you do, just go right now and order it off of Amazon. Shameless plug, but I have an Amazon storefront with all of the books that I've been reading that help with mindset, marriage, and getting closer to God. Here is the link:

https://www.amazon.com/shop/
fearlesslyshannon

Ok so back to fasting. Here are 9 reasons why we fast, or rather why we should be fasting.

1. We fast in obedience to God's word.
2. We fast to humble ourselves before God and obtain His grace and power.
3. We fast to overcome temptations in areas that keep us from moving into God's power.
4. We fast to be purified from sin (and to help others become purified as well).
5. We fast to become weak before God so God's power can be strong.
6. We fast to release the anointing to accomplish His will.
7. We fast in times of crisis.
8. We fast when seeking God's direction.
9. We fast for understanding and divine revelation.

I guarantee you that you need fasting because you need at least one of these 9 if not all of them. Just going through this book alone gave me so much revelation that I knew I needed to fast for my marriage. There are so many things that are unseen in this world. We don't see the spiritual warfare going on around us, or going on inside of our spouse. In my personal situation, I knew that something was more off than normal in my husband, and reading through this fasting book really opened my eyes to what could be and most likely is happening in and to him. I know every case is different. Maybe your husband cheated, maybe he got fired and lied about where he was going every morning for the past 3 months, maybe he has some literal demons inside of him trying to destroy your marriage. Regardless of what is going on, fasting will break down those spiritual attacks.

I'll leave you with one last thing that Mahesh says in his book. "Victory is only found in the realm of the Spirit, and that is why the devil takes every opportunity to divert us from the mode of prayer and fasting back into the natural mode." That is beyond accurate, because the devil will take the tiniest little bit you neglect, and he will pry open that door. After I got back from the women's conference, I was so happy and filled up, that I let my guard down, just a tiny bit, and he came at me full force breaking out all the stops. So much so that I had to get others involved to pray for me to get ahold of myself. When God really has something that is meant for you, and you finally step into that, it shakes Hell. It almost reminds me of how in the Disney movie Hercules, Hades gets so frustrated when he throws all he can at Hercules and it still doesn't go the way he wants it to. He screams, and his blue flame hair turns red with rage. I'm pretty sure, more or less, that's how the devil is when you find what your purpose in your marriage is. He really doesn't want you to fight for your spouse to come back. He doesn't want you to rely on God while praying and fasting and submitting to what God wants for you. He wants to break you. He wants to break your spouse. Don't let him. You have to stand up and let the devil know that He's ALREADY been defeated. That God HAS the victory. P-E-R-I-O-D.

If you were looking for a sign, here it is. Stop wallowing, stop worrying, stop whining. Start getting very diligent in your prayer life. Start fasting, and find out what God wants YOU to do. Maybe you are supposed to let your husband go. Maybe that's what God wants for you because He has already dealt with your husband and there is no changing him. Maybe God wants you to hold on a little bit longer because He is moving massive mountains for you right this very moment. The only way to find out is through prayer and fasting. No more excuses, you can start right now, or in the morning when you wake up. If you want answers, If you want victory, If you want God to lead you to where He wants you, then it's time to make these two things your priority. Let God worry about your spouse, you just worry about getting closer to Him.

In the meantime

eleven

Patience is a virtue. Although it's a super annoying one, it still is a virtue. Basically, virtue means something that is really good. Obvious? Yes, but I had to look it up because I wasn't sure what virtue actually meant. Now that I do, we can move on.

I've been told my whole life "Shannon you need to be patient." This would be said to me almost daily. Whether it was because I had to wait my turn for the restroom at school, wait in line at Six Flags, or wait to open Christmas presents. It felt like all I did was wait. Now that I'm in my 30s I realize that God was grooming me all along to learn to wait. It's not easy for me, and I don't like it. But it usually always works out in my favor when I do wait. Life is funny like that, and God has a sense of humor. But He also wants what is best for us, and if it was up to you or me, we'd hurry things along and end up with way less than what He had for us in the first place.

It's almost like hearing restaurant reviews for a new spot in town. You hear all these things, see pictures, videos, and the long lines outside. You wait months and months to get a spot at a table, and instead of waiting, you pay some guy named Brad a huge tip, more like a bribe, and you get into this place only to be disappointed by tiny, bite-sized pieces that you can barely taste. Then after this 5-course meal, you end up heading across the street to get a giant burrito from a food truck. Then you think to yourself "why didn't I just wait?" You should have waited to see if the food was good or to see if anyone you actually knew liked it. No, you just had to get ahead of yourself, and then you hated the outcome. That is exactly how some of us live our lives.

Right now, as you're reading this book in your hands, or possibly listening to an audiobook if I actually became that cool, you've probably been in a season of waiting. Maybe it's been a few days, a few weeks, months, or even years. Regardless of the time, you are stuck waiting. It's awful. It's probably the worst part of this whole thing. That's how I've been feeling, and I think that's exactly why I started writing this chapter. Subconsciously I KNOW that good will come from waiting. Yet, I feel like a 4-year-old child throwing a fit because I don't want to wait to have my dessert after dinner. I want it now. Although I'm pretty sure you know exactly how I'm feeling right now, I'm still hoping you can relate. We've all heard the saying "Good things come to those who wait." at least once in our lifetime. And while I believe that is mostly true, I still have a hard time following through with it.

When my husband first walked out, I was talking to a friend of mine who has been through a lot of the things I've gone through in my marriage, and I really trust what she has to say because she has a lot of wisdom. I look to her when I have any spiritual questions. If I ever feel like I'm straying away from God, I ask her to pray for me or give me some words of encouragement. Find someone like her to help guide you. Anyway, I was telling her what had happened and what was currently going on in my life and she told me something that stuck with me to this day. She looked at me and said, "Shannon, I really believe that God isn't giving you strength to leave him, but I think He is giving you the strength to stay with him." At that moment, I didn't get it. I WANTED to stay with him. I was broken that he left me and all I wanted was for him to come home. I couldn't even imagine how I could possibly not want him to come back into my life, my home. He took up all the space in my heart.

I remember one day while I was walking my dog outside I was just talking to God. I said, "God if you bring my husband back to me, I'll wait forever if I have to." Man, I did not realize what I was saying. I'm not saying that I regret that. I love my husband, but as I said, God has a sense of humor, and He also loves making us wait. So here I am, 11 months later, still waiting. Waiting on answers, waiting on him to come home, or miss me, or call me. I've moved away from all the anger, and I really just miss him. So I did what we humans do best, and I got super impatient. I know, shocker right? Look, you're probably in the same boat. Maybe you're waiting on answers too, or an apology, or just to hear his voice on the phone again. Not knowing what is going to happen is so hard, arguably the hardest thing about separations. This isn't my first breakup, but it is my first marriage and my first separation. How am I supposed to do this? How am I supposed to wait so long? Part of me doesn't even know how I've made it this far. I constantly wonder if my husband realizes how long he's been away from our kids. Does he know how long he's been away from me? I'm sure he does, and I'm sure it's hurting him. But these are real things that we think about. These are things that God hears from us all of the time. What's funny is, He isn't wondering when we're going to stop complaining, or being angry, or bored. He knows that once we get what He has in store for us, we're going to be so insanely happy that it'll be worth all the prayers He has heard us say. God can wait. We, on the other hand, have issues waiting. So how do you wait? Well, I can tell you that there are things you can do, things you shouldn't, and things that'll happen in the meantime.

The first thing that you need to know is that the devil is a punk. I heard Real Talk Kim say this so many times, but it's so true. He's basically a short bully who wants you to fail at life because he failed. So he will do everything in his power to get you to trip up, especially in your season of waiting. If he can get you to mess up the wait, then he wins and you...well you lose. Shannon, what does that even mean? Ok well in case you still haven't figured out what that means, let me tell you some things that have happened in my season of waiting.

When I say that the devil will pull out all the stops, I truly mean it. Here's the thing, whatever God has for you after your wait, is epic. We don't have a God that does small things. Everything He does is amazing, well thought out, and planned. So don't for one second think that whatever it is that He has for you is anything less. You know who else knows that fact? The devil. So if he can get anything in front of you to distract you, he will. He may not know exactly what God does have for you, but he does know that whatever it is, will make the very depths of Hell shake if you get to it.

For a long time, I've known this to be true about my life. Ever since I was a little girl, I've had obstacles, hardships, dreams, and a strong-willed attitude. God doesn't make us who we are by accident. He knows that when Jessica grows up she's going to be quiet and smart, perfect for whatever God has planned for her life. God knew that when I was made, I'd be loud, vocal, strong-willed, and I'll fight for what I believe in. I knew I was meant for something much bigger in this life. So if the devil can knock me off of my game, then I can't win. That's by his logic anyway, not God's. The enemy is smart. He's a lot smarter than what we give him credit for, not that he deserves it, but he's smart enough to know how to get us to fall into temptation. That temptation, pushed in front of us at just the right time, can completely derail God's plan for us. We have to be the ones to make sure we're strong enough in God's word that we can fight it. As I've said in a previous chapter, my weakness is feeling loved or wanted.

Now I want to make something clear before moving on with what I'm about to say. Just because you're a Christian, just because you believe in God, just because you may or may not know what He has planned for your life, DOES NOT MEAN that you won't get sidetracked. I've known from the VERY beginning of my husband leaving me that it was God's will for us to be together. That he would in fact come back home transformed. God promised that to me, then confirmed it with many dreams and through many people. But you need to know that even if God promises you something, if you don't put yourself in the position to receive that promise, and you try to do things differently, that promise may not happen. I have a responsibility to hold on to what God told me and to stay in my lane. So of course the devil knows this, and he's going to come at me hard. He's going to hit me until he knows one-thousand percent that I'm not backing down and I'm sticking with God's promise. You will trip up, you will make mistakes, and you will second guess what you think you "heard" from God. That's the enemy's plan. He wants you to lose your trust in God and in yourself. Don't let that happen. Try as hard as you can to keep pushing forward, and don't give up. Now that I've made sure you know this I can move on and tell you how I've been attacked this month.

Once I got back from the women's conference that I went to, you know, the one where I got full confirmation that my husband is coming home and I need to chill out and wait. Yea, that one. Well, once I got back I was set on waiting. I wasn't super sure what that wait would look like, but I knew that he'd come home eventually. Then, in swoops the devil, like the sneaky little snake that he is. I ended up going through a whirlwind of a weekend that almost knocked me flat on my face.

I had some family in town because one of my cousins was getting married. We had 10 people staying at my house and it was amazing.

I was surrounded by loved ones that I hadn't seen in a while, and we were about to have a great time at the wedding. I went feeling super cute, dressed up, and ready to have fun with my family. We had an insane amount of rain and my hair was soaked along with my entire outfit, but that didn't stop us from being happy and enjoying the day. Now, look, I didn't go to this wedding with a date or an intention of leaving with one either. Man oh man, did the devil have a plan. This very attractive man showed up with his cousin who was a friend of my cousin and asked me to dance. My family pushed me to dance with him because they didn't see any harm in it. They all knew what had been going on with my husband and me, and in reality, they just wanted to see me happy. So I took his hand and we danced and talked and laughed. He was kind and courteous, definitely a gentleman, so I thought. I'll get to all of that in just a minute. This was by far the best wedding I had been to in a very, very long time. I really don't think that I stopped smiling once that entire night.

Somewhere around 8pm, after dancing, eating, and talking a lot with this guy, he asked for my number. He wanted to talk and get to know me more. Stupidly I gave it to him. Knowing what I did, knowing that my husband would be coming home, granted I didn't know when I should have left it on the dancefloor. But I didn't. I gave him my number, and as he was leaving the wedding he asked me to walk him to his car. I'll spare you the corny details, but he went in for a kiss. I hadn't kissed another man in over 10 years, and I hadn't kissed anyone at all since my husband left. I felt weird. It felt odd. Not because it was a kiss with another guy, but because it felt EXACTLY like my husband. I don't mean like they kissed the same, I mean like I had to open my eyes to double-check that it was this guy and not my husband. I ended up pushing him away and saying goodnight. I went back to the wedding and we kept dancing for a few more hours.

I didn't know what to expect, or where this was going, if anywhere at all. The Holy Spirit was definitely trying to get through to me when I could only feel my husband when I kissed this man. That was God's first nudge to me, and I didn't listen. Well, it could have been the second nudge, he really resembled my husband and when we danced all I could think about was "wow I miss dancing with my husband like this". So the kiss thing was for sure the second attempt of God trying to make me pay attention. But again, I wasn't really listening. The next day this guy ended up calling me in the afternoon and things got really crazy. Now here is where it's about to get weird and maybe a bit messy so I'll try to not tell this confusingly, but I really want you to pay attention to the attack that is about to happen.

The devil started a few weeks back with this whole plan that was about to mess up my entire mindset, and of course, I didn't realize it until it messed me up. So before this wedding guy actually called me that day, I had another little plot against me. Now pay attention to the details ok, because like I said, he's a sneaky snake. This was a Sunday, the wedding was Saturday night, and being that it was two hours of driving, and many hours in the cold and being wet and dry and dancing and standing to sitting and eating and back to dancing again, we were all worn out. We all ended up sleeping in the next morning and missing church. Now I love going to church. I love surrounding myself with God's word and His Spirit. I believe in a real relationship with God, not a strict schedule, and the devil used this to his advantage. Seeing that I didn't start my Sunday morning off with worshiping the Lord like I normally do, I was easier to attack. All of a sudden I get this friend request, completely out of the blue and totally unexpected, from my ex. You know, the one that I was engaged to before I met my husband. Yeah!! I was shocked. I hadn't heard from him in over 10 years and I had no clue what was going on. He ended up reaching out because he was getting divorced, and ended up pouring out his heart to me. ELEVEN YEARS after dumping me. Ok weird. Then the wedding guy calls me and we start talking and I find out he's married. Not separated, fully married with a daughter.

At this point, my day has gotten totally thrown off track and I'm angry and upset. First of all, I will not now or ever be the other woman. I know how it feels to lose my husband, and all I could do at that moment was yell at him. I asked him how he would feel if he found out his wife was doing the same thing. I told him that she doesn't deserve to be treated that way and that he was completely disgusting to me. Did that hinder him? Nope. Not even in the slightest. He proceeded to tell me that he was falling for me and he couldn't get me out of his head etc. Weird right? I ended up blocking his number, then he found me on Facebook. I blocked him there. Then, crazy pants texted my cousin telling him he's basically in love with me. It's been a few weeks now, and I haven't heard a peep since but it was absolutely ridiculous. Don't worry, the fun isn't over yet. My ex-fiance proclaimed his love for me and I had to set him straight as well. I felt bad for him though because I felt like he was going through what I had before. I knew he felt alone, so I took this scheme that the devil was using and I turned it around and gave God all the glory. I tried as much as I could to help him see that God wasn't the one leading us together, but that he needed to run to God and not fall for an old flame, A.K.A. me. We ended it on a good note and it was turned around. It was a situation that the devil really tried to take me down with.

In the time that he was confessing his love for me, I started to have all these feelings resurface for my ex-best friend, the one I talked about a few chapters back. I truly loved that guy but had never told him, and a few months back when we ended up talking again, I had still never said a word about how I felt before. I started to freak out. I mean I was really freaking out. I ended up falling off all social media, staying in bed, not eating, and overthinking my entire life. Why? Because when the devil can't destroy you, he distracts you. He most definitely distracted me. I was in a bad mood, I wanted to lunge myself at this guy. I even texted him, nothing bad, just randomly in the middle of the night. Insert facepalm gif right here. It was cringe-worthy, but nevertheless, it happened. He ended up drinking that night so I let him go, and then God did what He does best and he shook me until I realized what was going on. I was letting all of this get to me. The wedding guy, the ex-fiance, and the ex-best friend. Three men, in one weekend. I was a mess. The enemy thought he had me until I proved him wrong.

Your job is to recognize when you're being attacked, and either let him attack you or fight back. Your waiting period may not be as eventful as mine has been, or it may be even crazier. Either way, you have to get as close to God as possible so that you have the discernment in your spirit to let you know when something isn't right. The Holy Spirit will guide you if you listen, but if you choose to do what you want instead of what God wants, that is when you'll get messed up.

In Proverbs 14:8, in the New Living Translation, it says "The prudent understand where they are going, but fools deceive themselves." and in the English Standard Version it says "The wisdom of the prudent is to discern his way, but the folly of fools is deceiving." If you are spending time in His word, God will give you discernment. If you're not sure what that means, discernment is the perception in the absence of judgment to obtain spiritual direction and understanding. It's God's little nudge, or shove in my case, towards the way you should be going.

When Santos, my husband, walked out on me, I had a choice to make. Either I could fall into the deep end, or I could dive into God's word and find out what God wanted me to do. I highly suggest the latter. Make a commitment to yourself and to God to get to know His word and His plan for your life. This past weekend we had a guest speaker at our church, Pastor Sterling Hudgins, and he said "You need to learn to yield to the spirit. If you can't yield to God, He can't progress you. So stop letting the world take you one way when God is trying to elevate you." God only wants what's best for us, and we always think we know what "best" is, but in reality, we have no idea how great God really is. His best is nowhere near our best. It doesn't matter what you feel or what you think, what matters is what you know God said about you.

Like I said, I knew from the beginning that God was going to bring my husband home, and my job during my waiting period was to have spiritual growth and to write this book. My job is to share my mess so that other women know how to navigate their mess when they're going through it. The entire world may tell you to run one way, while God is telling you to walk the other way. You are meant to do something great in God's kingdom. We are called to be the salt and the light on this earth. But we can't be a light if we are letting darkness control us, we have to lead by example. Following God is usually going to be the unpopular thing to do. While everyone is telling you that your husband doesn't deserve a second chance, he'll never change, and that you can't have a future with him, God may be saying the complete opposite. You don't deserve salvation, but God sent His one and only Son because He loves us that much. Saul was a terrible man who killed Christians just for believing Jesus was the Son of God, yet he changed and became an amazing man of God. God can and restore all things, so don't let anyone tell you what He can and can't do. You might think you can't do this, or that God messed up when He chose you to do what He's called you to do. I know the feeling all too well, I second-guessed writing this book, but I'm trusting Him. He called me to do this for a reason, and if it even helps change the trajectory of one person's marriage in the kingdom, then I'm all for it and it's all worth it.

When you start to get weary and think that you can't do this, or that you don't know if you are the right person for the job, think about Esther. God placed her in the King's presence to save His people. She was scared. It terrified her to say anything to the King, she figured that if she said anything he might kill her. God had big plans for her, "Then Mordecai told them to reply to Esther, 'Do not think to yourself that in the king's palace you will escape any more than all the other Jews. For if you keep silent at this time, relief and deliverance will rise for the Jews from another place, but you and your father's house will perish. And who knows whether you have not come to the kingdom for such a time as this?" (Esther 4:13-14 NLT)

How awesome is that? God created her for a specific time. He knew who she was, how she would act, and what would come of her faith when she acted on it. It's the same for you. God knows what you are going through, but He also knows what you can and can't handle. Trust me, sister, He gave these battles to you because He knew that you wouldn't crumble. He knew that you would help others get through their season because you were able to get through yours. You are going to lead so many people to God, just by living your life for him. Just by being an example of love and forgiveness, people will start to wonder why your situation is different. It'll be your job to talk about how God is getting you through it all. "It's time for us to step up and start accepting God's assignments, you can't stand still and climb higher" - Lynette Hagin.

It's time to start getting into a position for what God has for you. I can't tell you that your marriage will be restored, but I will tell you that it CAN be. God can do anything. He can bring your husband home and change him into the Godly man that you deserve and need. He can restore your marriage and make it better than you ever imagined. He can let your marriage end in a civil divorce that doesn't cause chaos and bring a new spouse to you who will lead you to do your purpose. I don't know what will come from your separation, but I do know that while you're waiting to find out, you need to dive into God's word. Get as close to Him as you can possibly get. Feeling lonely? Reach out to God. Feeling sad, mad, or upset? Talk to God about it. Pray more, read more, listen more. God is waiting on you. He might be waiting on you to stop the nonsense and follow Him so He can show you where to go next. He may be waiting for you to forgive your spouse. He wants you to reach out. You can't annoy God, He wants you to talk to him. Talk to Him about everything. That's what prayer is for.

"Don't worry about anything; instead, pray about everything. Tell God what you need, and thank Him for all He has done. Then you will experience God's peace, which exceeds anything we can understand. His peace will guard your hearts and minds as you live in Christ Jesus." (Philippians 4:6-7 NLT)

No fear, no shame

twelve

Going along with this entire book and why it even exists, I really need to touch on fear and shame. I don't feel like I can end this book without it. I've really been praying and asking God for wisdom on what you need to be getting out of this book, fear and shame came to mind.

As Christians, or being humans in general, fear comes very naturally to us. We're afraid of what we don't know, afraid of what we do know, afraid of what people might say about us, or that what God promised us may not come to pass. I remember reading a book about overcoming fear, and I really thought that I wasn't afraid of anything. Oh to be young and dumb. I was looking at physical things. I've jumped out of an airplane at 14,000 feet, so I'm not afraid of heights. I moved across the country with no friends or family around, so I'm really not afraid of big changes either. I always put my life on social media, because I'm not afraid of the opinions of random people. I really only knew of two things that scared me, spiders and small dark spaces. I'm still working on those, and sometimes I forget I'm even afraid of spiders when I see one of my kids screaming in terror. I'll just run up without thinking and kill it to protect them. No, Shannon isn't afraid of much at all. Well, let me just say that God will let you know when you're lying to yourself, and I was doing just that. I finally realized I had a fear. I was afraid of being abandoned. I was so scared that maybe, one day, something might happen, and my husband would walk out on me. Mind you, this was over 3 years ago that I was reading this book. I had no idea what was in my future, but it terrified me.

When God brought it to light that I really was afraid of something, I started to panic a bit. I started to overthink, and instead of giving this stupid fear over to God, I decided to take things into my own hands. Looking back on it now, it's crazy to think about. My fear became a reality. Could it have been prevented if I had let go of that fear and given it to God? Maybe. I'll never know, but the truth is fear is a liar.

At that moment, I was so scared that my husband might leave me one day, that I became almost sure that it would happen. I placed my faith in fear, instead of in Jesus. This is your wake-up call. Ok, you may be thinking, I can't be afraid of that because my spouse already left me. Well, how about this? Are you afraid that he won't come back home? Or maybe you're afraid that when he does come back home, it'll go right back to the things that made him walk out in the first place. A whole bunch of new fears ran through my head after the thing I feared most actually happened.

God doesn't want us to freak out about our circumstances. He wants us to trust in Him completely. Trust His promises. Trust His word. Trust that He knows how this is all going to turn out for you and that He really does know what's best for us. In The Message Bible, I truly love how it shows us our promises from God are a sure thing. "Whatever God has promised gets stamped with the Yes of Jesus. In him, this is what we preach and pray, the great Amen, God's Yes and our Yes together, gloriously evident." (2 Corinthians 2:20 NLT) If God promised it, it's going to happen. Why? Because our God can't lie. I know it's hard to trust the unknown, but it is possible. Sure you'll need to work on that trust, but all God ever does is for our good. So why doubt him?

I titled this book Laugh Without Fear because of my favorite verse which is Proverbs 31:25 "She is clothed with strength and dignity, and laughs without fear of the future." This is the type of woman and wife that God wants us to be. Women are strong, God knows that, and most of society knows that. But it's biblical to be strong, and hold onto your dignity at the same time. When the world wants us to throw frying pans across the room with our mascara running down our face, God tells us to have a noble character. I've had my fair share of insane moments, and I'm sure you have as well, it's normal. Women are pretty emotional creatures. Only you know the things you've done when you let your emotions run wild. We don't always think first then act. When we get hurt and we start living life by how we feel, we tend to act first and regret it afterward. We usually act out of fear, and then that brings on our shame.

What a perfect segue into talking about being ashamed. Fear and shame go hand in hand. It might not always seem that way but it really does. You do stupid stuff or say stupid things, and then you later regret it. There is so much guilt that we bottle up and it convinces us to hide from God. I've been there. Trust me, after my Golden Nugget, and then the worst wedding date in the world, I felt immense shame. Sometimes we feel like when we mess up we can't run to God. Like He's going to push us away and say "I don't love you anymore, you're terrible." No! Our God is so much better than we are. He might not be particularly happy with what you've done, but He's not going to turn you away if you just come to Him humbly and say "Dad, I messed up, I need help, I don't know how to fix this." Through this journey that I've been on, there is a song that helped me when I really needed it. It was most definitely God talking to me when I felt so awful about not waiting it out like He told me to. God promised my husband would return, and out of fear, I tried to find comfort in anything but His promise. I acted out of fear, then felt so ashamed it almost crippled me. I walked outside, ready to cry, and I started to talk to God. Apologizing and ready to give up, the song Crazy about you by Plumb came on. In case you haven't heard it, I want to share some of the lyrics with you because God is saying this to each of us when it comes to our shame.

> *You screwed up, made mistakes. Got dirty from the messes you've made. But I whisper "That's okay, I love you, despite what you say". Take another chance on my love. No matter what you've done right, no matter what you've done wrong. You've been fighting for so long, You belong in my arms.*

How beautiful is that? Those lyrics broke me down in the middle of my backyard, and I couldn't stop crying. I've heard that song so many times before, but it never touched me the way it did that day. It felt like God reached down and grabbed all that shame and pulled it right out of me. He doesn't want us to carry that around with us forever. Once you repent, He erases that sin and says He won't remember it or bring it up again. God is doing the same with your spouse, maybe this is your time to see that. Maybe you keep telling God "Well my husband did all this and he should be ashamed. Why doesn't he feel bad? Why isn't he guilty?" Truth is, we don't really know, and I know that I've already touched on this a little, but it's really pressing on me to reiterate it right now, so one of you isn't quite getting it yet. Sometimes we need to hear it a few times before we get it. I know I'm like that, many people are. If you're anything like me, then you might need this repeated as well.

Following God doesn't mean that you'll never be afraid, that nothing will ever come to scare you, or that you will feel amazing no matter what you do. There are going to be plenty of times that we are scared or feel a large amount of shame because we know we didn't do what we should have, or we did something we really shouldn't have. In those times, God wants us to run as hard and as fast as we can into His arms. It's wild that we have someone who wants us despite all that we do wrong. God is our protector and our comforter. We just have to remember that while we're an emotional basket case. Much easier said than done, yes, but that is why you have to spend time in God's word. Study it, and let God use it to speak to you and guide you to where you need to go. God knows when you're being stubborn or acting out of emotion. He knows exactly what you need to hear when you need to hear it.

This week I've been taking my own advice. I started praying and fasting. I've been fasting social media this whole week, and as crazy as that sounds, it is really hard. Some of you may not need to get rid of it because doing so wouldn't really be a sacrifice, but for me, it was and is. In giving that up, I realized that I was placing it in front of God. That's no bueño, my friends. God has to go first. Instead of waking up and getting on social media first thing, I started waking up and spending time with Him. This life isn't going to be easy and there are so many things that we have to be afraid of or ashamed of. Spending time reading your Bible is going to show you so many ways out of that state of mind. We have to start focusing on Jesus and not on the world. Nothing is as important as being with Him.

All of those other things can wait. Fear can wait. Shame can wait. Laundry and social media can wait.

When you step back and look at what everyone says about fear, you know, False Evidence Appearing Real, it's easy to see that it's not important. Jesus is the truth, fear is the lie. The truth is more important. Who really has time to listen to lies? The enemy wants you to be tempted by everything else so that you'll ignore your bible. He wants you to dwell on your shame, he wants the guilt to eat you up and devour your heart and mind. He wants you to think about anything other than what God wants you to focus on. Your guilt is a big thing that the enemy uses to get your mind off of God. If you feel enough shame, you won't run to God, instead, you'll hide from him. None of these things are new to God though. He's seen and heard it all and guess what? He still wants you to run to Him. You might have flaws but you are STILL worthy of His love and forgiveness.

I want you to think about a different perspective on feeling ashamed that I didn't really think about until someone brought it up. You can feel ashamed and the devil does play on that. If he knows he can keep you down by making you feel even worse about what you did, then he'll use that. He uses whatever he can to get in, and once he's in, he'll try to destroy your relationship with God. But what if you aren't feeling terrible about what you did? Usually, when you sin (or your spouse sins), you feel shame. Sometimes you don't. Sometimes you justify it. Yep, you justify sin. That is another chokehold for the enemy. But why? Because sometimes when you sin, you fear the truth. That truth being, YOU messed up and YOU were wrong.

We can be so afraid of the truth because of our pride. Pride will kill you. Pride will keep you so far from what God has planned for your life, and if it keeps you far from God, then the devil is all about it. Satan is great with his mind games. He'll get you to think things like "it wasn't that bad" or "it's really not that big of a deal other people do it all the time". He's a storyteller, so he'll spin things inside of you so that you lie to yourself to feel better about what you did, even if you feel bad at that moment. He'll use lying as a coping mechanism. Paul said "But I am afraid that as the serpent deceived Eve by his cunning, your thoughts will be led astray from a sincere and pure devotion to Christ." (2 Corinthians 11:3 NLT) The devil will mess with your thoughts. Paul is just warning you to be on guard. It won't always sound like an attack from the enemy, usually, it sounds like our own voices. That is where it gets tricky. The word tells us to stay aware because we can easily fall into his traps. Guilt can be good or bad. We need to be able to acknowledge the bad things to repent. Once you've admitted those things to God, there is no reason to stay in that shame. If we can never even admit to ourselves that we've messed up, then we can't repent, and that will have an effect on our salvation. "For Godly grief produces a repentance that leads to salvation without regret, whereas worldly grief produces death." (2 Corinthians 7:10 NLT) God lets us know there is a difference between worldly guilt and Godly guilt. If we run to him He'll let the veil be removed from our eyes, we'll see the truth, and be able to live in freedom. (2 Corinthians 3:16-17 NLT)

We're all going to have temptations. Temptations to sin, or get distracted, or feel any other way than how the bible tells us we should feel. No one is exempt from that. "The temptations in your life are no different from what others experience. And God is faithful. He will not allow the temptation to be more than you can stand. When you are tempted, he will show you a way out so that you can endure." (1 Corinthians 10:13 NLT) You'll be able to get through whatever it is that you feel bad for, so will your spouse. But there is no reason to feel shame for it at all, but you will. The closer you get to God, the more conviction you'll feel when you do wrong. That's a good thing. When you start to feel guilty for something, that is your proof that you're becoming more Christ-like. God knows when you feel that shame, but then He will wipe that away. The devil, on the other hand, turns that into keeping you down for good. He wants you writhing in pain thinking about fear and guilt. Frankly, I think that's pretty low of him, but again, he's a punk so you can't really let your guard down.

I want to share a few different verses with you that'll help make the devil look like an idiot. Fear and shame don't belong in your heart, and though it's hard to shake those things, it's possible to get rid of those feelings. So I'll give you a few on fear and a few on shame. Read these, then write them on sticky notes and stick them all over the place. The more you remember what God says, the easier it'll be to fight those thoughts and yell "NO" to fear and shame. While I'm at it I'm going to put another song in front of you. The song is No Shame by Tenth Avenue North and it goes like this:

> It might look like I'm broke but I'm healing. I'm learning to bring everything that I'm feeling. No shame. So forgiven man, it's hard to explain it. I'm finally living with no shame. I look in Your eyes, full of tenderness, and it doesn't make sense. You see me just as I am, and I'm never too much. Lord I gave you all my blame, You gave me a new name.

When you were saved, God made you new and He gave you a clean slate. He created an open-door policy so that if you needed anything, or wanted to get rid of anything, He was always ready to hear what you had to say. Time and time again, He'll remind us how much he loves us. And love doesn't hold onto fear or force anyone to feel ashamed of who they are or what they've done.

What God says about shame, guilt, and fear:

- Because the Sovereign Lord helps me, I will not be disgraced. Therefore I have set my face like a stone, determined to do his will. And I know that I will not be put to shame. (Isaiah 50:7 NLT)
- Most of you opposed him, and that was punishment enough. Now, however, it is time to forgive and comfort him. Otherwise, he may be overcome by discouragement. So I urge you now to reaffirm your love for him. (2 Corinthians 2:6-11 NLT)
- Those who look to him for help will be radiant with joy; no shadow of shame will darken their faces. (Psalms 34:5 NLT)
- Fear not; you will no longer live in shame. Don't be afraid; there is no more disgrace for you. You will no longer remember the shame of your youth and the sorrows of widowhood. (Isaiah 54:4 NLT)
- For God has not given us a spirit of fear and timidity, but of power, love, and self-discipline. (2 Timothy 1:7 NLT)
- Such love has no fear because perfect love expels all fear. If we are afraid, it is for fear of punishment, and this shows that we have not fully experienced His perfect love. (1 John 4:18 NLT)

> - This is my command, be strong and courageous! Do not be afraid or discouraged. For the Lord your God is with you wherever you go. (Joshua 1:9 NLT)

No matter what it is that is holding us back from running to Him, there is verse after verse to help us see that God doesn't hold our fears or mistakes against us. He knows how you feel, He just wants you to stop running away from him, and start running to him. Maybe you are in the spot I was a few years ago, maybe you think that you don't have anything that you're afraid of. It might seem like you're totally fine, but I really think you should pray and ask God to show you what is buried inside of you. I heard someone say once that when you're afraid of something, you can't trust God, and if you don't have real trust in Him then you're doubting what He can really do. I never thought I would doubt Him, but when we don't trust Him that's exactly what we're doing, we're doubting. So I want you to pray with intention, let Him search you, and expose the truth. This isn't so that you'll have more things to fear, but instead be able to put your full trust in him, so that even if these fears happen, then Satan won't make you trip and fall, because you already know you've already given it all to God.

I've read many books that have additional prayers that'll help during moments like these. So I've decided to add one right here at the end of the chapter so that you can pray with intention to let God search your heart and make you aware of any fear or shame inside of you. You don't have to pray this out loud, but if you can or are up to it, I really recommend you do so. Our tongue holds the power of life and death, and when you pray out loud, it helps break any hold the enemy has on you. When you pray, believe in what you are saying, and know that God does hear every word.

Dear Lord,

Please search my heart. Expose anything that I may fear, anything that I'm afraid to let come to light. I don't want to feel ashamed anymore of the mistakes that I've made, nor do I want to let my pride get in the way of what You want for my life. In order to get rid of that guilt, I have to give it to you. I want you to take my fears and my shame, and give me the wisdom that I need to overcome it all. Show me in ways that I'll understand, and keep the enemy from bringing them to me over and over again. I'm done with fear and shame. I know that with you there I can overcome all of it. Give me strength, and let me feel your love even deeper now.

In Jesus name, Amen.

thirteen

Have you ever looked up what the word Epic means? Yea, me neither. But since I decided to title this chapter Pretty Epic, I thought that I should probably figure out if I'm using the word correctly. There are a few definitions of this word, but I'm going off of 2a and 2b from Merriam-Webster.com. This is what it states for Epic, Extending beyond the usual or ordinary, especially in size or scope, and/or heroic.

Now, I don't know about you but I feel like the word Epic really does describe our Lord, Jesus Christ. He did some major things while He was here, and is still doing some pretty epic things now, through the Holy Spirit and His people. Jesus epically came to the earth, through a virgin. Then He died an epic death, for every one of us so that we could be saved and forgiven and be with Him in Heaven. Then He made some even more epic moves, rose back to life, and completely shocked the devil, and all who doubted Him. His whole life here was one giant epic tale, yet we still have a hard time believing that God will move in epic ways in our own lives.

He did so much, He died for people who would never even love Him because He is the epitome of love. Yet we think for some reason, being a child of God, isn't enough for Him to do some massive things in our lives. It's kind of insulting if you think about it. He did so much for you, yet you don't believe He can still do more. But God doesn't do things because you deserve it. He does things because He loves you with all of His heart. We throw around the saying "I'd die for so-and-so" when we are trying to explain how much we care about them. But you may never have had to actually go through that for somebody else. Who knows if you would actually give up your life so someone else could live. Until you've been in that position, it's all just words. They aren't just words for Jesus. Our God actually did that for us, He laid His life down for you and me. He could have easily walked away from being beaten and crucified, but His love for us was stronger than any pain that He had to go through. So you don't think He'd fix those things that are broken in your life just because you asked? Our God is the God of signs, wonders, and miracles, and He wants to give them all to you. All you have to do is trust that He will. In Hebrews 2:4 it says "And God confirmed the message by giving signs and wonders and various miracles and gifts of the Holy Spirit whenever he chose." That verse is all you need, to see that these things are yours. So it's your job to trust that He will, all you need to do is ask. Ask God to move in your life, ask Him to make some big things happen in your life. Yes, it's that simple. But here is the catch, you have to prepare for it, and you have to expect it.

During some bible study time, I came across some verses that really opened my eyes to why God does what He does. Everything He does has purpose and reason. Let's go into The Message Bible and read 1 Corinthians 26-31 "Take a good look, friends, at who you were when you got called into this life. I don't see many of "the brightest and the best" among you, not many influential, not many from high-society families. Isn't it obvious that God deliberately chose men and women that the culture overlooks and exploits and abuses, chose these "nobodies" to expose the hollow pretensions of the "somebodies"? That makes it quite clear that none of you can get by with blowing your own horn before God. Everything that we have—right thinking and right living, a clean slate, and a fresh start—

comes from God by way of Jesus Christ. That's why we have the saying, "If you're going to blow a horn, blow a trumpet for God."

I love these verses so much because sometimes we ask God "why me?" and right here is that answer. He chose you on purpose so that people who knew you, watched your situations, and watched everything you had to go through, will end up seeing what God does in your life. People who grew up so poor that they had to share a cup of ramen, became CEOs of million-dollar companies. Women who've been abused, leading thousands on how to overcome that. Horrible men who were drunk, on drugs, and left their families, turning around and being on fire for God. God can and will take any situation and turn it into something that no one saw coming.

A lot of the time, we look at our situation and wonder why we couldn't have been born into a rich family. Or why those 5 other entrepreneurial ventures didn't work out for us, but your friends from High School are doing great with them. I mean if God wants to bless us then why doesn't He just do it right away?! I've thought about these things before, I'm sure you have also, but here's the thing. We weren't created to live selfish lives. We weren't put here so that we could have the best house, the coolest cars, all the handbags our hearts desire, and the perfect relationship that everyone envies. What would that do? Who would that help? Now, I'm not saying that God won't give you all those things, He just might. To be honest, the people who do have those things, or appear to have those things, aren't always truly happy anyway. God wants to use broken, hot-mess people, and take them to new levels because it'll have a ripple effect on so many. Your situation may affect people so deeply that they'll run to God with open arms, and share Jesus with others.

God does some major things in crazy ways. They don't always make sense to us at first, but there is always a reason for them. God wants the glory, but sometimes people try to brag on themselves and say it was all them that did it and not mention God at all. And that my lovely friends, is why He tends to do things that are so wild, that there is no way we can take the credit. I want to go over a few different accounts in the bible that show how awesome God is and how He loves to do crazy, epic things. I'm not sure where you are in your walk with God, maybe you read your bible every day, maybe you only read it on Sundays at church along with the Pastor. Maybe you picked up this book because you have no other options and you don't know what to do anymore since your spouse left, and you're not even sure you're a believer at all. No matter where you're at, you can always use some clarification. The few passages that I'm going to share with you are easily found in the bible. I'll tell you the books and/or verses to find them, and I encourage you to read them yourself because you could get something out of them that I'm not bringing to the table. Either way, these are great examples of the insane things that God does for His children. Things that we never think could happen to us in real life, but definitely have happened. God will never look at you and think "Yea I don't think they deserve something epic to happen in their lives. They're not worthy." No!! God wants you to know you are so worthy. You're worthy of all His love and His grace, and His amazing miracles. He has something for your life. A purpose that can change your life and someone else's, but you have to trust Him in the process and know that it won't always look like the best outcome. It may feel painful and pointless, but God always has a purpose in whatever you're going through.

- Rack, Shack, and Benny -

The first epic story I want to talk about is how God took the faithfulness of three boys, Rack, Shack, and Benny (major points to you VeggieTales fans), and did something that you normally see in movies. These three dudes were under King Nebuchadnezzar. They were always faithful to God and the King knew this. King Neb ended up having this massive golden statue of himself built and set up for everyone to see. Now, I'm sure you've seen statues of other historical figures before, and ok it's not that big of a deal, but King Neb took it a few steps further and wanted this thing to be worshiped. He went so far as to make it a law, that the moment they heard the sound of any kind of music they had to stop what they were doing and bow down and worship immediately. Anyone that didn't, would be thrown into a human-sized furnace and be burned to death. As I'm sure you can imagine, this new rule terrified people. They didn't want to die, obviously, so they listened and they bowed down to the golden statue. It didn't matter what they believed, how old they were, man, woman, child, they just didn't want to die. I get that, it's a crazy rule and personally, one that I think sounds stupid, but this King didn't think it was dumb at all and was willing to kill over it. Well, Rack, Shack, and Benny didn't worship the King's gods, and definitely were not going to bow down to a golden statue of him. They loved the Lord with all their hearts and knew that the God of Abraham was the only God worthy to be worshiped. They refused to bow down when they heard the music, and even when they were threatened with being killed. This made the King super mad, they worked for him and he knew them as good men, so he wanted to give them one more chance. King Neb had the guys brought to him and he asked them himself because he was shocked that they wouldn't bow down. So he was like "look, the music is gonna play again so whenever you're ready just bow down real quick and I'll act like you didn't blatantly disrespect me the first time! And if you still don't bow down then I'm just throwing you all in this furnace right here, right now, and there isn't any god who can save you." (these are my words obviously, but it really puts it into perspective in today's environment).

Well, the boys weren't having it and stood firm in their faith and belief in their God. They straight up told the King "Look we don't answer to you, and we're not bowing down to your statue. The God we serve has the power to save us from you and your furnace, but even if He decides not to, we're still not bowing down to your statue or any of your gods!" The King was enraged, even more, he really thought that he convinced them and then they basically chose death over bowing down. So he screamed at his men, told them to make the furnace 7 times hotter than what it was currently at, then to tie the boys up and throw them in. The furnace was so hot that the men who threw Rack, Shack, and Benny into the fire were killed by the flames because the furnace overheated. Can you picture how mad the King had to be to not even care that his own men died right there just trying to throw these guys in? But then God did what only God can do. The king ends up yelling and asking if they only threw in three guys who were tied up. So not only did the King see someone walking around in there with the boys, but they weren't even tied up anymore. He could tell that they weren't even hurt and the other man he saw walking around, had a light radiating from Him. They end up coming out of the furnace unharmed, not burnt at all, and not even smelling like smoke. That had a ripple effect on the King and his people so much that he ordered that anyone who spoke against their God would have their limbs ripped from their bodies. Then he ended up promoting all three of them.

If you want to read about this on your own go ahead and read Daniel chapter 3. God took these normal young men, had them in a crazy situation, and used them to bring God all the glory. They couldn't brag that they did any of that. There's no way they could have spun that story into something it wasn't, yet it was something that impacted so many people. People in that time in that kingdom, other kingdoms, and years and years later. They were so confident that God could save them if He wanted to but brave enough to say that even if He decided not to. They still believed and trusted in Him no matter what. We have to learn to be that bold because God always protects His own. When you read that story, the things in your life right now don't sound as out of reach anymore, do they? The circumstances that you are asking God to change, actually seem like they can change. You may feel like you're going through a fire, but you're not. Nothing is too big, too crazy, or too far out for God to fix. I love this chapter so much because it really shows us how much we should trust God. Be bold in your faith and trust in Him. We might let Him down, but God will never let us down.

Let's look at another epic story in the bible, shall we? I want to really help you understand that the God we serve does big things. It doesn't matter who you are, how much money you have, how many followers you have on Instagram, or what kind of car you drive. God chose you because He loves you and He knew that He could use you and do major things in your life if you would just follow His instructions and trust Him. That being said, we're going to talk about a very well-known event, David and Goliath.

- Slingshot to the face -

The story of David and Goliath has been told so many times. It's in kids' books, it's used by motivational speakers, and of course, it's a VeggieTales movie. But it dawned on me that maybe there are still a few people who haven't heard it, or haven't heard real details about it. Growing up, before I ever went to church I had heard the story as well. A young boy defeated a huge giant with a rock and a slingshot.

He had faith in his God and with faith, you can accomplish any task no matter how big. That's about all I knew.

But I want to give you a good background on this event. Now Goliath was a huge dude. There has been a lot of debate on how tall he actually was because measurements and translations were different from what we understand nowadays. But regardless, his height isn't what I'm trying to get at here. He was somewhere between 7 and 12 feet. That's a pretty large estimate, but all the scholars can worry about that. No matter how big he was, we know he was big enough to scare an entire army. Israel and the Philistines were about to go to war with each other. But Goliath came out from the Philistine army and yelled out to the Israelites. Basically, he said that instead of the entire army fighting, all they needed to do was send out their best soldier to fight him. If Goliath wins, the Philistines will take the Israelites as slaves, and If the man that Israel sends wins, the Philistines will surrender to them. Pretty good deal I think, but Goliath was so intimidating that these guys stayed there on the sidelines, not sending anyone, for 40 days. Every single day, Goliath walked out and yelled the same thing, but they still had no one brave enough to fight him. That was until David showed up.

If you know anything about David, at this moment in time he was just a teenager. A young dude, who took care of sheep. He wasn't even supposed to be anywhere near the battlefield, but he had a few brothers who were following Saul, so David's dad sent him down there to check on his other brothers and take them food. By the time David got there with everything his dad sent him with, Goliath was making his appearance for the day. Trying to see if anyone would come out and fight him. Still, all these soldiers were terrified. When David heard Goliath going on and on, he got kind of mad. He's like "Who is this dude who is yelling at God's army? Is he crazy?" (again my translation, but you get it right?!) David didn't get why no one would go out and fight this guy. So he took it upon himself to do it. He went to Saul and said he'd go out there. Saul freaked, and was like are you serious right now, you do see this guy right? Sometimes I wish I could have seen this in real-time, David was like "Look I take care of sheep and I've had lions and bears come after them and all I had was a slingshot and God helped me defeat them, how is this any different?" So Saul was like "ok, May God be with you but take all this armor so you can be protected."

David, remember a teenager, was like yeah I can't wear all this stuff, I'm good with my slingshot. Goliath saw that David just had the slingshot and looked at him and said "Do you think I'm a dog, coming at me with sticks?". He scoffed, laughed, and mocked David. Right about now, I'm betting David looked crazy to everyone else. No sword, no armor, no military training. Just some crazy kid running after this giant scary dude. But again, God is just awesome, and He was ready for something epic to happen so that it would bring God all the Glory.

So David looks at Goliath and responds (in my words) "You come at me with all your weapons, ready to fight, but I come with the God of Israel, who you mocked. He will deliver you into my hands today. Not only am I going to kill you but I'm gonna cut your head off and everyone will know that God doesn't need a sword to fight and win". Sure enough, that's what happened. When everyone else saw this massive man, they were terrified, but David only saw how massive God was. He knew he couldn't lose as long as God was with him. So he went after Goliath, knocked him out with a slingshot right to the forehead, then killed him and cut his head off with the dude's own sword. How crazy is that?! David was running on his faith in God and it paid off big time.

He was a nobody. He wasn't in the army, had no real training, and to top it off he wasn't even paid attention to by his brothers.

He just loved God and trusted that He would be with him in battle. You can read the entire story for yourself in 1 Samuel chapter 17. David used his faith, and God moved epically. God started with this faithful teenager and transformed him into a King later on in life.

Sometimes we can't see the bigger picture. We don't think we're enough or that there is any way that God could use us or our story to help someone else. I can promise you from personal experience, that God chose you for right now. You weren't born by accident. You grew up where you were supposed to be with the people you were supposed to. Maybe some things have happened in your life that weren't exactly according to God's plan but don't think for one second that He won't use what you've gone through to do something amazing.

I can only speak from my personal experience, I don't know what is meant to happen with you and your spouse. I can't promise you that your husband will come back, or that you'll have a perfect marriage after you're finished reading this book. I can't tell you what God has for your life right now, but I can tell you that if you seek out the answer, God will tell you. I've seen so many things on walking away from your spouse after infidelity, or fights, or how the woman should be strong and never submit to a man and you should be independent. I realized that listening to the world is what put me in the place that I was in, to begin with. I've learned that whatever the world is telling me to do, is usually the opposite of what God wants me to do.

God won't hate you if you end up divorced. God won't walk away from you if you end up staying in your marriage. God loves you more than you could ever love Him back, and he knows the right way to handle any situation that you're going through.

Right at this moment, it has been 15 months since my husband walked out on my kids and me. Everyone has told me to walk away and file for divorce because there's no way he'll change or come back. I've been told that I've seen sign after sign of why I should just give up on my husband. I've been told that what my husband has put me through, gives me every right by the bible, to leave him. I've been told to go on tinder or try to date around (although we all know how that golden nugget went). I've been hurt, I've cried, I've screamed until I lost my voice. I've been told to go get a "real job" since my husband can't be counted on. I've watched my kids' hearts get broken, and seen them be abandoned by his whole family. I've watched them cry and beg me to take them to see daddy. I've seen my husband drunk, possibly on drugs, gain and lose weight because of being depressed. I've seen the bags under his eyes, because I know he's not getting sleep. I've heard him promise the kids things that never happened. I've had friends tell me how terrible my husband is doing at his job and how they can tell he's not doing that great since our separation. I've had dream after dream, confirmation after confirmation of what is going to happen, what has happened, and what will come as long as I trust God and His process.

In 15 months I've learned who I was as a wife and who God wants me to be. I've learned that it's ok to fall and mess up as long as you learn, grow, and don't stay in that same place. I've been able to let go of all the anger that has held me captive for so long. I've learned to truly understand the meaning of "let go, let God". I put my full faith and trust in Jesus Christ, and He has fully taken care of me and my kids. My husband never stopped putting money in the bank, I was always taken care of. I never had one bill past due. God blessed my business so that I was able to give back more to my church. I was able to go on three different vacations, tithe way more than my 10% because I wanted to, have food on the table, bless others, start a website, and write this book that you're reading now.

When you decide to follow God, it's going to look crazy to everyone else. It's probably going to look crazy to you if we're being honest. Everything I've gone through and done since my husband has left has "looked" like the wrong thing. I know without a doubt that God is moving big mountains right now. I know what God promised me for my family and my marriage and until He tells me otherwise I'm staying put right where I am. I know that God does big, epic things, and I know that He can and will do them with me. You should be believing that He can and will do the same with you. You took a big step when you decided to run to God after your spouse left. You could have run to the world for comfort. You could have done what you wanted to do. It's your life after all. Instead, you chose to follow God's plan.

Maybe you'll write a book and help others going through what you have had to endure. Maybe you'll speak to a room full of High Schoolers and help them set up a future running full force after God. Maybe you'll create a podcast that helps women learn how to be the Godly wife that the world tells them not to be. Maybe your spouse will come home, maybe you'll get divorced. But please, whatever you do, remember that God has something huge for you. All you have to do is trust Him with everything that you have. He will get you through this trial, stand with you in the fire, and defeat your giants. Our God is so good, and this is just the beginning of what He has for you.

God has clothed you, with strength, dignity, honor, and wisdom. He has given you all that you need so that you can look to the future and laugh because you know that He's got your back. You don't have to be afraid, even when everything seems like it's exploding right in your face. He's right there, holding your hand, patting you on the back, and opening doors that you haven't yet walked through. So put on your armor, because it's time to take your stand. No one, nothing, no circumstance can stand against you when God is on your side.

I want to thank you for taking the time to read this book. I truly hope that there is something in here that has helped you and what you're going through right now. I pray that God guides you and restores all that the enemy has tried to take away from you. He can only take what you give to him, so don't let him take any more. If you ever want to share your testimony, a story, or how this has impacted you please feel free to message me on Instagram or send me an email. I'm going to leave you with one last prayer that you can say right now. If you're new around here, or if you've been saved and born again for years, it's great either way. Pray it as often as you feel you need it. You can never over-pray, trust me God loves hearing from you.

Dear Heavenly Father,
I ask that you come into my life right now, and cover me in your love. I believe you love me so much that you died for my sins on that cross, and then rose from the dead just so I could be in Heaven with you someday. Lord, I ask that you give me the strength and courage to get through everything that the enemy is throwing at me right now. Guide me into what you have purposed for my life and my marriage. Give me the wisdom on how I should handle (spouse's name) leaving. I know that I'm not perfect, but I thank you for your heavenly grace. Please search my heart, and my intentions, and bring to light anything that is not of You. I want to live for You Lord, and I want to do Your will. Thank you for guiding me, loving me, and never leaving me. I'm ready to fully trust in You and Your plan

for my life. Take care of (spouse's name) while we go through all of this, protect them from the attacks of the enemy, and give them an intense desire to want to get to know You and your word.

In Jesus name, Amen

Don't think that you have to be a perfect Christian or even a perfect wife. Perfect only exists through Jesus and we can't ever reach that. However, God looks at our hearts and knows how much we are trying to be the best we can be. Only He knows what is going on inside of you and inside of your spouse. Since our God is the God of truth, if you ask Him to give it to you straight, He will.

I don't think marriage was ever meant to be easy, but neither was being a follower of Christ. I do know that He will give you all that you need to overcome what you are going through. No matter how your marriage continues from here on out, God will always love you. Take this book with a grain of salt. These were all my experiences, and you should always look into what you believe God is telling you to do, or not to do. Don't ever feel bad if you get things wrong, or mess up a bit. It happens to the best of us. Sometimes we think we know exactly what God told us to do, and we end up being completely wrong, I know I've been there myself. Other times we get it spot on, but then we have to commit to trusting Him to do what He promised.

Now it's your turn to put into action what you've learned from this book. Maybe this is your second chance, it's time to be the wife that God would be proud of. Just remember, there is always a purpose in your pain, it's never for nothing.

MARRIAGE, DIVORCE & REMARRIAGE - KENNETH E. HAGIN

FORGIVING WHAT YOU CAN'T FORGET - LYSA TERKEURST

WAIT AND SEE: FINDING PEACE IN GOD'S PAUSES AND PLANS - WENDY POPE

WHEN WOMEN PRAY - T.D. JAKES

THE HIDDEN POWER OF PRAYER & FASTING - MAHESH CHAVDA

31 PRAYERS FOR MY HUSBAND - JENNIFER SMITH

WIFE AFTER GOD - JENNIFER SMITH

About The Author

Shannon Jimenez can usually be found with a book in her hand on how to become the best possible version of herself. She spends her time coaching women to learn to love themselves from the inside out, and inspiring them to live more bold and fearless lives. More recently, she's been the content creator and blogger over at laughwithoutfear.com, where she tries to keep things as real and as positive as possible, while learning to live her life unafraid. Her biggest motivators in life are her faith and her two kids, and they're the reason she decided to write her debut non-fiction book, Laugh Without Fear.

Currently, Shannon lives in St. Louis with her family and her golden retriever, Simba. Going on new adventures is one of her passions, so she travels as often as possible. If she had it her way she'd be living on the beach under a palm tree drinking out of a coconut. She'll always have pineapples on her pizza, and won't be caught dead using wet napkins. She's fluent in Spanish and sarcasm and is a professional at pointing out the obvious. She believes that life is meant to be lived to the fullest with lots of laughter, love, and little to no negativity.

Acknowledgements

So many people have been by my side through all that I've gone through and I couldn't have become who I am without you guys. I want to take a moment and thank each of you for all that you've done for me, because the support I've gotten with my separation, and with my book means the absolute world to me.

K & T - You guys have helped me get through all of this more than you know. Having people who know what I'm going through but who can also give me wisdom in different ways has saved me from disaster so many times. Just knowing I can run to either of you for guidance, Godly advice, or just knowing you'll both be completely honest with me has affected me so much. You have a strong marriage and a strong family and I'm honored to be able to come to you whenever and know that you'll always give me the answer that is aligned with God instead of the world. Thank you for everything you've done for me.

Mark & Danielle - I'm still not fully aware of what I did to find friends like the two of you. Ever since I can remember you both have always been there for me, no questions asked. Knowing that you're both always there to back me up, stand with me, and help me the second I ask, has made me feel more than loved. It's rare to find friends like you guys, so I know I'm beyond blessed to have you in my life. Thank you for being my bodyguards, drivers, protectors, helpers, and for making it beyond clear that no matter what I can always reach out to you guys. Thank you for making sure I'm included and never alone.

Kristoff - It's been such a long road for us. I know that we don't always see eye-to-eye but I do know that we will always love each other like family. God put you in my life for a reason, and I know 100 percent that if you weren't there for me through this whole separation, I would have broken into millions of pieces. Thank you for always believing in me. You know how big I dream, and sometimes I need to be brought back down to earth. You know when I need a spiritual slap, and when I just need to cry. No matter how far apart we are, how long we go without talking or seeing each other, or whether or not we agree, you will always be my soul sister. I love you beyond words.

Crystal, Sasha, & Brittany - This is the best friend group I could have ever chosen. I don't understand how we're all so different, yet we all work so perfectly. Without our group chat and girls' nights, I think I'd be a lonely mess. You guys let me vent whenever I need it, and you never once judge me. I'm so thankful for you guys and your kids being in my little family's life. You've made sure that my kids feel so much love, support, and pure happiness and I can't even begin to explain how grateful I am for that. Moms don't always agree on how to raise kids, but you three are moms that I'll always take advice from. Also a special thank you to Jordan and EJ because life wouldn't be as funny without you guys. When most people would tip-toe around my feelings, you two were there making fun of me and still making me feel normal. Thank you for always letting me be a mess, then helping me get back up.

Megan - I'm so happy you're in my life, and I know you came back just in time. We've been through so much together and you have watched my family grow, learn, and go through good times and bad. Thank you for making my kids feel like they're a part of your family. I'm so happy to be a part of your growing family now as well. Thank you for always being honest, but still letting me spread my wings when I need to. Sometimes I just need to be sarcastic, laugh, and talk in only gifs (without being told I'm weird lol) and you are the one person I know I can always turn to for that.

Pastor Mark - I'm so grateful that you're so blunt and honest. Without you being the way you are, I would probably be in denial and always think that I'm in the right. I've made so many mistakes and messed up more times than I can count, but You've always accepted and loved me while still telling me exactly how God feels. Thank you for never sugar coating the Bible, I'm honored to call you my Pastor.

Lembach - You were never actually my teacher in High School but you definitely had the biggest impact on my life. Even though I hated it at the time, you taught me about maturity and character. You gave me real-life advice at a time when I needed it when no other teacher would, and I truly believe that helped me get through the past two years with class, grace, and dignity. When you signed my yearbook you left the quote "It's not about the adversity you face, but how you overcome the adversity that you face." It took me so long to understand that. Then once I started really going through all of these trials, I realized that I can choose how to act and how to carry myself through it all. Thank you for believing in the weird kid in the gym.

Mom & Esty - I'm not going to make this one too sappy, but without you two I have no idea where the kids and I would have ended up. You both have always believed in me and shown me love and support. You've reminded me how strong I am, and how much of a great mom I am to my kids. You let me laugh, cry, and be weird whenever I need to be. I'm so happy and thankful that the kids have always had you guys to lean on and run to. I know that if they didn't have you guys, things would be very different than how they are today. You two are my rocks and I love you both with everything I have in me. I'm happy God gave me you.

XOXO, SHANNON

www.ingramcontent.com/pod-product-compliance
Lightning Source LLC
Chambersburg PA
CBHW050331010526
44119CB00004B/122